Enemies of Choice

Enemies of Choice

The Right-To-Life Movement and Its Threat to Abortion

Andrew H. Merton

Beacon Press • Boston

Copyright © 1981 by Andrew H. Merton

Beacon Press books are published under the auspices of the Unitarian Universalist Association, 25 Beacon Street, Boston, MA 02108

Published simultaneously in Canada by Fitzhenry & Whiteside Limited, Toronto

Printed in the United States of America

(paperback) 9 8 7 6 5 4 3 2 1

Library of Congress Cataloging in Publication Data

Merton, Andrew H., 1944-
    Enemies of choice.

    Includes bibliographical references and
index.
        1. Abortion—United States—Moral and
religious aspects. I. Title.
HQ767.3.M47   363.4′6   81-65762
    ISBN 0-8070-0485-5 (pbk.)   AACR2

To my mother and the memory of my father

Acknowledgments

I wish to thank Steve Getlein, Sue Hertz, Debi McDermott, and Kathy Scrizzi for research assistance; Barbara Ehrenreich, Frances FitzGerald, Don Murray, and Ron Winslow for suggestions and encouragement; Vivian Noble, Patricia Weil, Roger Wall, Linda and Tony Mauro, and Joan and John Felder for their hospitality and patience; and Joanne Wyckoff, my editor at Beacon Press, for recognizing something others did not. Special thanks to my wife, Gail, a writer and editor by trade, for her resolutely honest criticism, and for temporarily suspending her career to become a full-time mother, giving me time to write. (Everyone named above does not necessarily agree with all of the views I express in this book.)

Others—too many to name here—helped in various ways. I thank them all.

Contents

Prologue

Let us start with the end—the end which members of the right-to-life movement will employ a wide variety of means to achieve. The end, or goal, is not simply to stop late abortions—third-trimester abortions in which the fetus is nearly fully developed—although a casual look at right-to-life propaganda might indicate otherwise; the movement churns out millions of leaflets, brochures, cartoon books, and posters bearing photographs of bloody fetuses aborted late. Nor is the goal simply to put a stop to all legal abortions now performed in clinics, doctors' offices, and hospitals. What the right-to-lifers have in mind encompasses far more than that.

They want to achieve their end through a proposed amendment to the Constitution of the United States:

> The paramount right to life is vested in each human being from the moment of fertilization without regard to age, health or condition of dependency.

The goal of the movement, then, is nothing less than the preservation of anything unborn and human, including zygotes. A zygote is an egg at the moment of fertilization. The version of the so-called human life amendment cited above is sponsored annually by Senator Jesse Helms of North Carolina and Representative Robert Dornan of California. There are other versions; however, the only significant difference among them is that some make an exception when the life of the mother is endangered. All of them accept, without question, the right of each zygote to develop into an adult human being. Thus it follows that the vast majority of right-to-lifers wish to outlaw not only abortions, but certain birth control methods, notably the intrauterine device (IUD) and low-estrogen pills, which allow fertilization to take place but prevent implantation of the zygote on the uterine wall.

Opponents of abortion have been forced into this extreme position by the fact that fertilization is the only decisive, easy-to-pinpoint moment in the development of a human being. If they were to concede that this single cell were qualitatively different from the creature that might grow from it, they would be lost, since there is no other precise point during the development of the zygote into an embryo, the embryo into a fetus, to which they can point and say, "Here—here is where personhood begins." Philosopher Richard Werner inadvertently points out the impossibility of this task in a paper entitled "Abortion: The Ontological and Moral Status of the Unborn." Werner is essentially against abortion, but argues that it is morally acceptable if done before the fetus becomes sentient. ". . . the best science of the time," he wrote in 1974, places sentiency "at between 8 to ten weeks of pregnancy . . ."

And what is the maker of laws supposed to do with such an inexact calculation? Is it eight weeks, or is it ten? Or do we split the difference and call it nine? And if a doctor is accused of aborting an eleven-week fetus, how is it proven, particularly since the process of abortion itself destroys the evidence?

And so, the zygote. Those who believe that a zygote is as deserving of protection as the born human being—that to kill a zygote is as much murder as to kill a child—usually make any of three arguments. The first is entirely based on physical evidence: the zygote, based not on what it will eventually become, but on what it is at the moment, is deserving of protection; it is, after all, human. Here it is crucial to distinguish between two meanings of "human being"—that is, human in the purely genetic sense, and human in the sense of being a person, with full moral rights and responsibilities. The right-to-lifers tend to blur this distinction, or disregard it altogether. Thus, a note appended to the text of the Helms-Dornan amendment quoted above explains:

> "Each human being" is used to avoid any confusion about whether there is a distinction between "person" and "human." In order to have the right to life vested, it is necessary only to be a human being. Once this right vests, there can be no quibbling over whether or not "personhood" attaches, because only human persons have the right to life. That is, artificial persons (corporations) do not have a right to life under the 14th Amendment.

The point of the note is that, to the sponsors of the amendment, it does not matter that a zygote has no consciousness, reasoning power, sense of self, capacity to communicate, or any number of other qualities normally associated with personhood; the fact that it is human in the genetic sense alone is sufficient to grant it the right to life. A prominent proponent of this view is Dr. Jack C. Willke, president of a nationally based organization called the National Right to Life Committee and author of "Handbook on Abortion" and other antiabortion material. In a taped speech entitled "Abortion, How It Is," Willke says that when the sperm and the egg join,

> we have at that instant created a new living being. Judge this being to be human at that moment or not, we cannot deny the biologic fact of the total uniqueness of this new living being, a new being that is not at the end of the line, but at the dawn, a new being containing within him or her self the totality of everything an old man or woman will ever be, a new living being that is programmed to live eight and one-half months within the mother and as many as ninety years without.

Essentially, Willke confuses the blueprint with the building—for the genetic code contained in the zygote is exactly that, a blueprint; the finished product is yet to come. Do we equate the discarding of a blueprint with the destruction of a building? No, and one suspects that at some level Willke is aware of this. While he rarely travels without a collection of photographs of aborted fetuses, it apparently does not include a dramatic shot of a dead zygote. (Indeed, right-to-lifers usually avoid the term "zygote" altogether, preferring the more emotionally loaded "fertilized egg"—just as they prefer "unborn baby" to "fetus.")

The second argument is more sophisticated: some right-to-lifers believe that the zygote should be classified as fully human in the moral, as well as genetic, sense, not for what it is, but for what it might become. The zygote differs from an inorganic blueprint because, if nurtured properly, it might grow into a person. The most eloquent and frequent defender of this point of view is John T. Noonan, professor of law at the University of California at Berkeley. The presence of the genetic code, together with the *potential* for rational thought, he argues, is enough to earn the zygote the same protection an actual person enjoys.[1] This point is hotly disputed by those who favor retaining legal abortion—philosophers such as Mary Anne Warren who argue that the rights of any potential person are outweighed by the rights of *actual* people, i.e., pregnant women.[2] (Among other things, Warren and Noonan disagree about the meaning of the word "person.")

The third argument contends that the zygote's claim to inviolability lies not within the physical sphere but in the realm of theology. For example, in his book *Abortion and the Meaning of Personhood*, Clifford E. Bajema goes to great lengths to trace the development of the fetus, only to conclude:

> The biological facts are impressive, but they are not sufficient to totally convince everyone that the human person begins at conception. There are some who believe (myself included) that personhood is a spiritual concept, not meaningful without reference to the relationship between God and man, and not ultimately explainable except in a "theological context."

It turns out that by "theological" Bajema really means "Christian." Bajema further weakens his argument by conceding the following:

> Does the Scripture ever really say that what is sexually conceived by man is from the moment of conception *man?*
>
> The answer is "no" if one is expecting Scripture to provide a *scientific statement* on when individual man begins. The answer, however, is "yes" if one is expecting Scripture to provide a *theological understanding* of man from the point of his beginning to the point of his end.

The extent to which religion permeates the right-to-life movement is such that an occasional atheist in the ranks is cause for celebration. Many antiabortionists, whether Catholic or Protestant, are fundamentalist. They declare that only God can create a man, and therefore only God has a right to destroy a man. And by man, they take pains to point out that they mean fertilized egg: zygote. It bothers them that the Bible carries neither a specific injunction against abortion nor, as Bajema concedes, a specific description of zygote, embryo, or fetus as person. And they ignore considerable Biblical evidence that God does not, in fact, view the fetus as a person (see chapter seven).

None of the foregoing is intended to be the last word on the subject; it merely serves to point out that grounds for debating the personhood of the fetus—let alone the zygote—are many and varied. Yet, a powerful movement has grown up around the certainty of zygote as person. Most right-to-life literature presents this notion as fact—as something so obvious it need not be explored. The movement accuses anyone who condones legal abortion of, at the very least, standing by and doing nothing while millions of innocent human beings are slaughtered. The logic goes this way: (a) zygotes/embryos/fetuses are human beings in the fullest sense of the term, and therefore deserving of protection; (b) abortion kills zygotes/embryos/fetuses; therefore (c) abortion is murder, and (d) anyone who condones abortion condones murder. This line of reasoning naturally causes many proponents of abortion to become defensive—until they recognize the flaw in step a. Once that happens, it becomes clear that the right-to-life movement rests on extremely shaky philosophical ground.

The movement had its beginnings in the early 1960s. The first stirrings took place almost simultaneously in New York and California—the two states which, at that time, appeared most likely to liberalize their restrictive abortion laws. At first, the activists were virtually all Catholics, and the arguments they used against abortion were closely patterned after the church's arguments against artificial birth control.

Wherever sentiment for liberalization grew, the right-to-life movement grew to counter it—Colorado, Massachusetts, Michigan, Washington State. By 1973—when the United States Supreme Court decriminalized abortion—more than half the state legislatures in the country had considered bills to liberalize abortion laws, so antiabortion forces had already gained considerable experience at the grass-roots level. While the liberal reform movement tended to view the Supreme Court decisions as its final victory, the antiabortionists vowed that the battle had just begun.

From 1973 to 1976, the Catholic Church remained the most effective foe of abortion in the United States. The many local right-to-life groups that sprang up were actively encouraged by the National Conference of Catholic Bishops, as well as prelates on the regional level, such as John Cardinal Carberry of St. Louis. But during the late seventies the base of the movement broadened as fundamentalist Protestants by the hundreds of thousands became politically active for the first time. The movement found its political vehicle in the "born again" Republican Party—no longer the party of the moderate eastern business establishment, but now dominated by a coalition of Americans angered by issues as diverse as mandatory school busing and the easy availability of material they considered pornographic. By 1981, the movement had a friend in the White House and working majorities in both houses of Congress. Federal funding for Medicaid abortions had been eliminated, and there seemed a reasonable chance that Congress would send a human life amendment to the states for ratification within the next few years.

The movement has come this far on the strength of emotional appeal. Its propaganda is powerful, not logical; again and again we hear that legalized abortion in the United States amounts to a holocaust that makes the Nazis, by comparison, look like pacifists. It relies heavily on matters of faith; the Biblical injunction "Thou Shalt Not Kill" is extended to include fetuses, embryos, zygotes.

There is no doubt that most of the activists in the movement are sincere in their belief that abortion is murder. Yet it is likely that they have other motives—perhaps hidden even from themselves—which drive them; we shall explore some of these. There is considerable evidence, for example, that right-to-lifers are appalled by what they see as the rampant sexuality of today's society, and that they view the outlawing of abortion as a means of restoring a more repressive sexual climate. Similarly, most oppose the gains of the feminist movement—particularly the independence women have come to enjoy since the mid-sixties. They openly yearn for a return of women to the traditional role of wife and mother—something that is not likely to happen as long as abortion remains easily available. There are also considerable elements in the movement which are antidemocratic, antiintellectual, and antihumanist, and which view abortion, sexual freedom, and equal rights for women as the evil by-products of a society dominated by the will of man, rather than the will of God.

Thus, while the movement holds the fetus in high regard, it reserves a considerably lower place for women, humanists, and intellectuals. It is possible that right-to-lifers revere the fetus for reasons having nothing to do with its humanity: (1) It is harmless; having no ideology or power of its own, it is no threat to the movement, and (2) Its enforced presence frustrates the goals of the movement's adversaries.

Such speculation may seem cynical. Right-to-lifers would no doubt proclaim that their only reason for involvement in the movement is to protect the lives of innocent human beings. Yet I will examine a considerable body of evidence that makes it clear that, at some level, right-to-lifers do not, in fact, regard the zygote, the embryo, or the fetus as fully human.

In its emotional appeals and its disregard of logic, the right-to-life movement resembles many other oppressive crusades in human history, from the earliest witch hunts to the Spanish Inquisition to the Nazis' persecution of Jews and other *Untermenschen* (subhumans). All were based on false logic, and all resulted in widespread misery and loss of freedom. The right-to-life movement differs from these others only in subtlety; it does not directly name the objects of its ire—primarily women—but instead would set severe limits on their liberty in the name of saving fetuses.

This is not a book about abortion. Nor is it about people who might seek to limit abortion by some degree—those who see the need for some abortions but oppose, perhaps, third-trimester abortions, or even second-trimester abortions, except in the case of a severely deformed fetus. Rather, it is about the movement to stop *all* abortions, including those caused by IUDs and certain pills. It is, in short, about the supporters of a human life amendment.

While researching the right-to-life* movement I taped lengthy interviews with dozens of leaders and activists in the movement. The writings, public activities, and public pronouncements of right-to-lifers, together with those interviews, constitute the raw material from which this book was written.

---

*Some antiabortion groups prefer the term "pro-life" to "right-to-life." In this book the terms will be used interchangeably to refer to organizations and people supporting a human life amendment.

CHAPTER 1

BIRTH CONTROL
AND THE CATHOLIC CHURCH

Dr. Jack C. Willke's photographs of dead and mutilated fetuses are available to the public in slides, posters, and wallet-sized sets. They also appear in countless flyers, pamphlets, and booklets, as well as in "Handbook on Abortion," which Willke and his wife, Barbara, coauthored in 1971.

Some of these photographs are in color. In one of these, the purple torso of a fetus is displayed against a white background. Arms are still attached to the fetus. The two detached legs and the head are placed alongside the torso. Another photo shows two tiny, detached arms and two legs against a pulpy red background. Others show whole fetuses, bloody and discolored, aborted by hysterotomy or saline injection.

But many activists in the right-to-life movement say the photograph that affects them most deeply—the one they turn to when they feel their resolve to continue the struggle waning—is black and white. It shows four fully formed fetuses in a garbage can lined with a black plastic bag, and it is usually captioned: "The result of one morning's work in a Canadian teaching hospital." Activists call this "the bucket shot."

The photographs have made Dr. Willke a powerful man. Even his adversaries in the movement—and there are many—acknowledge that Willke's knack for propaganda (right-to-lifers use the term "education")—of instilling in the antiabortion constituency the true meaning of abortion at the visceral level—is unsurpassed.

In 1980, Willke was elected president of the National Right to Life Committee, the largest (and, Willke contends, the predominant) antiabortion organization in the country. In January 1981, less than a week after the inauguration of President Ronald Reagan, Willke was in the Oval Office of the White House, discussing strategy for outlawing abortion in the United States.

His rise to prominence has been dramatic. He has been involved in antiabortion activity for only eleven years. Before that, he was simply a Cincinnati, Ohio, physician with a thriving sideline in sex education.

He was born in Mariastein, Ohio, on April 5, 1925. Five years later, his family moved to Kneipp Springs, Indiana, where his father, Gerard, a physician, became medical director of a sanatorium. This sanatorium was run by nuns. For the next six years young Jack and his five brothers and sisters received their education in the form of tutoring from these nuns.

In 1936 the Willkes moved again, this time to Cincinnati, where Gerard went into private practice. Jack continued his education at Saint Claire's School and Roger Bacon High School. He attended Oberlin College, and then went to the Medical School at the University of Cincinnati. By the early fifties he, too, was in private practice in Cincinnati.

In 1948 he had married a nurse, two years his senior, and around 1953 the two of them began giving talks on the subject of sex. They were, they thought, ideally suited for the job. Both were accomplished public speakers. Barbara had taught nursing courses, and Jack, by his own recollection, had won every public speaking contest he had ever entered. In addition, they had what Barbara called a "spanking good marriage," and a growing brood of young children (there were eventually six). And they were devout Catholics. This last qualification was important, since they gave many of their talks at church or church-related functions. Their first audiences were Bible study classes. Soon they branched out into premarriage counseling, and then began talking to married couples about ways to teach their children about sex. Jack, tall and thin, with a pale reddish complexion and a receding hairline, always took the lead. His style was diffident and restrained. His speech was, and still is, peppered with Rotary Club folksiness; often his sentences begin, "Listen, guys and gals . . ." Barbara was the perfect mate, complimenting him, occasionally teasing him, filling in details. She was more robust and outgoing than Jack. Her disposition was unfailingly sunny. She had what was known then as an infectious giggle.

The Willkes worked well together, so well that word spread about their ability, and by the end of the fifties, they had delivered their talks all over the country, as well as in Canada. In 1964 they published their first book, *How to Teach Children the Wonders of Sex.* In a section entitled "Sex Is Sacred," they summed up their philosophy on the subject:

The act of love that we perform in marriage is a sacred

thing. We must realize this. Just think for a moment: if there were no sin in the world, when would the marital act be used? It would be used only between a loving husband and wife, in marriage, to express unselfish love for each other, to give each partner joy and happiness, and when God wills it, a child. Many have abused sex, certainly, but that does not change its basic goodness any more than the abuse of alcoholism [sic] would make thirst a bad thing.

Thus, for the Willkes, sex was good only in marriage, and then only if pregnancy were at least a possibility. Anything else, including birth control (which is not mentioned in the entire book) is sinful. And for the Willkes, there was always enough sin to go around. It usually went around in cars full of teenagers, and was particularly virulent at drive-in movies: "These should be banned for high school students unless the parents are in the back seat." Going steady, the Willkes said, was "morally dangerous":

This is said repeatedly, but we honestly think parents are not often aware of the true danger. There are always exceptions, of course, but the majority of teenagers who go steady find themselves each time "going a little further," and it is the rare young couple going steady who do not, sooner or later, indulge in sexual intimacies progressing from kisses, to touches, to—We should be quite blunt. Parents who allow their teenagers to go steady should realize the boy and girl face serious temptation, and that the odds are high that they will sooner or later sin together. We believe that such parents *share the responsibility* for their sin.

And with sin, of course, came guilt. It is worth quoting one additional passage from *How to Teach Children the*

Wonders of Sex to emphasize this point. In a section called "Masturbation" the Willkes tell nervous parents:

> When the time seems opportune, face up to the fact that in the early teens most boys begin to masturbate. This again is not for mother to talk about—it is for dad. It is often extremely difficult for dad to face this, the reason being that quite frequently dad may carry with him some guilt feelings from his youth about masturbation. However, this discussion is important, and no one can speak as effectively about it as a boy's own dad. You should explain that sex powers are holy and beautiful, and are not to be misused. The strong, mature man will learn to reserve these powers as his gift to his wife when he marries.

The idea here seems to be that fathers should conscientiously pass on their guilt to their sons. (Nowhere in the book is it mentioned that girls masturbate.)

It is significant that the Willkes viewed their philosophy on sex as somewhat progressive—a sensible, middle-of-the-road approach. Women of the Victorian age, they said, saw sex as a "duty, something of a necessary evil to be tolerated." On the other hand, they frowned on modern mores —"freedom to talk and act as we please about sex, denial of sin, of moral good or evil, complete liberty, or libertarian license for anybody." They had noticed the sexual revolution, and they did not approve.

On May 9, 1960, the U.S. Food and Drug Administration for the first time approved for general use a birth control pill for women. It was called Enovid. It was manufactured by Searle & Company, and it was available by prescription only. It was the most significant technological event in a decade during which the range of sexual behavior acceptable to a large segment of the American people (but not *all* the American people) broadened extraordinarily. The pill seemed the perfect equalizer, freeing women to enjoy sex when and with whom they chose without worrying about pregnancy. Although many states still had laws prohibiting the distribution of birth control materials to unmarried people, it was not difficult for a young woman to get a prescription. She had only to tell her gynecologist that she would be getting married in a month or so, and that she wanted to be protected on her wedding night. If a particular gynecologist balked, there were plenty of others who would cooperate. Particularly on college campuses, the sexual double standard was under attack. Through the 1950s, strict curfews were enforced at women's dormitories, and during the limited hours when men were allowed in the rooms, the rules of behavior often resembled those of a child's game. Both the boy and the girl were required to keep at least one foot on the floor at all times.

But during the sixties the curfews disappeared, as did the visiting hours and the children's rules. The traditional role of the college in loco parentis crumbled. By the end of the decade, coeducational dormitories were common, as was the phenomenon known as "living together," and communes flourished at the edges of college campuses.

In 1965 the United States Supreme Court declared unconstitutional an 1879 Connecticut law that forbade the use of contraceptives by anyone, including married couples. The ruling was important because it established a "right of privacy" for married couples, but in practical terms the court was simply going along with an established fact. The Connecticut law, and others like it, had been ignored and unenforced for several years. By 1966 it was estimated that six million American women—about one fifth of those of childbearing age—were using the pill.

The speed of the sexual revolution was such that many Americans, even some who considered themselves liberal, worried about an erosion of traditional moral standards among the young people of the country. In November 1965, Andrew Hacker, a professor of government at Cornell University, published an article in the *New York Times Magazine* entitled "The Pill and Morality," in which he speculated on a change in dating behavior brought about by the pill:

> For a long time there has been a certain ritual, not without moral overtones, connected with birth control as practiced by unmarried people, college students or not. The young man is "prepared" on a date; the girl is not. If there is a seduction, he takes the initiative; she is "surprised." If she succumbs, he deals with the prevention of conception—which is proper because she had no advance warning as to how the evening would turn out. Vital to the ritual is the supposition that the girl sets off on the date believing that it will be platonic; if it ends up otherwise she cannot be accused of having planned ahead for the sexual culmination. (Very few unmarried girls have owned their own birth control devices.)
>
> But now, for a girl to be "on pills" wipes out entirely the ritual of feminine unpreparedness. With the pill, one girl I talked with said, "you no longer have the ultimate excuse of saying no."

Hacker said he had surveyed a group of 200 freshmen in one of his classes and found, to his surprise, that the majority of girls, as well as boys, thought the university clinic should be willing to prescribe pills for undergraduate girls on request. Having said this, he apparently felt compelled to stress what he saw as the essentially monogamous nature of college women:

> Thus, when a majority of girls state they would like to have the pills available, it does not mean that they are about to embark on a nymphomaniacal orgy. Quite the contrary, it suggests that they wish to catch themselves a husband and simply desire to have both a sexual relationship and contraceptive protection during the period of engagement.

Tame and condescending as it was, this idea went far beyond the bounds of decency for a large segment of the American population. The sexual revolution flowed around these people, perhaps touched them, but did not move them. It was to this constituency that the Willkes addressed their books.

As it happens, there was a group of men—far more influential than the Willkes, though not nearly as influential as they themselves clearly hoped—who espoused the same conservative values, and who took the lead in fighting the sexual revolution and everything about it—particularly artificial birth control. These men made up much of the hierarchy of the Roman Catholic Church, both in Rome and in the United States.

Here it is crucial to distinguish between the Catholic leadership and Catholics, because in matters of birth control and abortion the flock paid little attention to the shepherds. Survey after survey showed that the use of artificial birth control was as widespread among American

Catholics as among the rest of the population. Even the church acknowledged that its members in America were disturbingly inattentive about such matters. In June 1960, before the pill was widely available, the National Catholic Family Life Bureau reported that Roman Catholic married couples were using birth control "in about the same measure" as Protestant and Jewish couples. The bureau's director, Monsignor Irving A. DeBlanc, called this finding "alarming, arresting, and provocative."

Throughout the 1960s the Catholic leadership waged a rearguard battle against birth control. The real conflict took place within the church itself—liberal theologians and prelates insisting that church teaching should be reinterpreted in a way that would acknowledge reality, conservatives not budging from the principle of "natural law," which, they said, artificial birth control would violate. The Reverend Joseph S. Duhamel, writing in the Jesuit magazine *America*, defined natural law as "the statement of the inner principles of action, placed in man by God in making man what he is, and demanded by the very nature of man so that his human activity may direct him to that perfection which is proper to his human nature."[1] A somewhat circular definition—the principles seem to demand the principles. In any case, under natural law artificial birth control was (and is) deemed wrong because it interferes with the natural, God-designed sequence of sex, or rather, one particular aspect of sex, which the theologians insisted on calling "the marital act." (Actually, the church had not even sanctioned "natural" birth control until 1930, when Pope Pius XII approved the limiting of births through the rhythm method.)

There were liberal forces at work within the church

during the sixties, however, and the man who gave them cause for optimism was Pope John XXIII, although judging from John's early pronouncements on the subject of birth control, one would consider his help extremely unlikely. In December 1959, for example, the pope took note of widespread hunger in the world, but warned against "erroneous doctrines and pernicious and death-dealing methods of birth control"[2] to correct it. In April 1960, during a Palm Sunday homily, he went further: "Don't be afraid of the number of your sons and daughters. On the contrary ask divine providence for them so that you can rear and educate them to their own benefit and to the glory of your fatherland here on Earth and of that one in Heaven."[3] But it was also John who convoked the Second Ecumenical Council in 1962, which gave rise to a lively debate on the birth control issue. In March 1963, Pope John instituted a commission to study the question; in 1964 his successor, Pope Paul VI, confirmed and enlarged the commission.

In the United States, one prominent and beloved prelate was particularly outspoken in his desire to see a change in the church's position. This was Richard Cardinal Cushing of Boston, who on a television talk show in 1965 expressed sympathy for "those people who are having problems with large families and who are worried sick about the church's teaching." He added, "I'm hoping and praying that all these problems will be settled by the Commission's report." Cushing was the only American cardinal who frequently remarked or implied that what couples did about limiting the size of their families should be a matter for those couples to decide.

The commission made its report to the pope on June 26, 1966. Had Cardinal Cushing been able to see it, he would have been pleased, for the majority of the members advocated "decent and human means of contraception," and said that birth control could contribute to fulfillment in marriage and to the "truly human life." The majority said of sexuality, "It is proper to man, created in the image of God, to use what is given in physical nature in a way that he may develop it to its full significance with a view to the good of the whole person."

There was also, however, a minority report, which declared contraception "intrinsically evil"—even though the minority members could not find anything in the Scriptures to back up this point of view. The minority argued that Catholics should continue to avoid artificial birth control simply because the church had always told them to, and it was unthinkable that the church had been wrong all these years. The following two sentences from the minority report suggest the panic:

If we could bring forward arguments which are clear and cogent based on reason alone, it would not be necessary for our commission to exist, nor would the present state of affairs exist in the Church as it is.

And:

For the Church to have erred so gravely in its grave responsibility of leading souls would be tantamount to seriously suggesting that the assistance of the Holy Spirit was lacking in her.

This amounted to thinking the unthinkable.

Pope Paul VI received the report in secret. Within the next year he made two pronouncements that hinted strongly that he was on the side of the minority. In October 1966 he told the Italian Society of Obstetricians and Gynecologists that the church's teaching with regard to birth control could not be considered "in a state of doubt," even though he had not yet made a definitive pronouncement on the subject. (When an issue is deemed in a state of doubt, Catholics are allowed to follow their own consciences in determining their conduct.) And in March 1967 the pope issued an encyclical entitled *Populorum Progressio* in which he lamented the deplorable condition of much of the world's population. "The world is sick," he declared. Yet he warned against any "attempt to check demographic increases by means of radical measures." By which he meant birth control. Then came a jump in logic which had become built into conservative Catholic thinking: "Where the inalienable right to marriage and procreation is lacking, human dignity has ceased to exist." Within the papal brain, there existed little distinction between the *availability* of birth control devices and the mandatory use of such devices.

Later in 1967, the third World Lay Apostolate Delegation, a group of Roman Catholic laymen meeting in Rome, approved, 67-21, a referendum endorsing artificial birth control. But the pope was not moved. On July 29, 1968, after conferring for months with the conservatives who had authored the minority report of his commission, he presented what was to be the last word on the subject, an encyclical entitled *Humanae Vitae.* The document reaffirmed the doctrine that Catholics could limit the size of their families only by the rhythm method or abstinence. As had been the case with the minority report, *Humanae Vitae* relied for its authority on church tradition, rather than on Scripture. Monsignor Ferdinando Lambruschini, who presented the text at a news conference, felt compelled to defend the church's right to interpret authentically "the natural moral law even if not based implicitly or explicitly on revelation."[4]

In the encyclical the pope said the widespread use of artificial birth control would promote immorality: "... how wide and easy a road would thus be opened up toward conjugal infidelity and the general lowering of morality." Young men, in particular, must not be offered "some easy means of eluding" observance of "moral law," he said. The pope viewed women as frail, vulnerable creatures: "It is also to be feared that the man growing used to the employment of anticonceptive practices may finally lose respect for the woman and, no longer caring for her physical and psychological equilibrium, may come to the point of considering her as a mere instrument of selfish enjoyment, and no longer as his respected and beloved companion." Thus, a man loses respect for his wife when he slips on a condom. But what of a woman on the pill? Does she begin to view her husband as nothing but a sex machine? The pope did not speculate on this.

In the encyclical the pope, mindful of the burgeoning world population, continued to confuse optional and mandatory birth control: "Who will stop rulers from favoring, from even imposing upon their peoples, if they were to consider it necessary, the method of contraception which they judge to be the most efficacious?"

This pronouncement was simply the latest in a long

series from conservative church officials who, since the late fifties, had been treating the population problem as though it were a sinister plot intended to undermine the church's authority in the area of procreation. This strain of paranoia was particularly evident in the United States, where, in 1959, the bishops took note of rising concern over the rate at which the population of the world was growing. In November of that year the bishops warned American Catholics against supporting any form of artificial birth control as a means of stemming the tide, and accused those who used the term "population explosion" of employing a "terror technique" to compel people to have fewer children.[5] In 1963, Monsignor George A. Kelly, official spokesman for family life for the New York Archdiocese, hinted that advocates of artificial birth control were actually advocating a gentle sort of genocide: "While supporters of the contraception movement may have idealistic motives, powerful economic, social, religious, and political factors are also involved—and the other peoples of the world know it. Latin Americans, Asians, and Africans suspect that they are told that they should stop breeding because they are bringing 'inferior' peoples into the world to outnumber the 'superior' whites."[6]

Throughout the sixties the American bishops engaged in an eerie sort of doublespeak when talking about birth control. Monsignor Kelly, for example, quoted Pope Pius XII: "The right of parents to have many children is a 'fundamental, personal right' bestowed by God—one with which no human institution should tamper." On the other hand, the right *not* to have children was substantially more limited: "... many husbands and wives are justified in practicing the rhythm method for medical, eugenic, economic, or social reasons."[7] "Many," of course, is a far cry from "all," and in any case the rhythm method, popularly known as "Vatican Roulette," was notoriously unreliable. In church thinking, then, to have many children was every couple's right; on the other hand, to limit the size of one's family was, in most cases, a wrong. Thus, the "right" to have children was not right at all, but a duty.

By 1965, the government of the United States was pouring millions of dollars into family planning efforts around the country. The Office of Economic Opportunity had aided community birth control programs in cities as diverse as Washington, D.C., Milwaukee, and Corpus Christi, Texas, as well as in many rural areas. A White House Conference on Health urged the government to provide birth control devices and instructions to all families in the country, but especially to the poor. And money from huge foundations was aiding the effort. The Ford Foundation alone parceled out $14.5 million in grants to various birth control research projects.

All of this did not go unnoticed by the bishops. In November 1966, more than 200 Catholic prelates, meeting in Washington, gave themselves a name: the National Conference of Catholic Bishops. The first official act of this new body was to unanimously condemn the administration of President Lyndon B. Johnson for seeking "to persuade and even coerce the underprivileged" to limit the size of their families. The bishops said the government led welfare recipients to believe that unless they used birth control, they would lose their benefits. The text of their statement included a sentence which they might well regret today, in view of the current debate on abortion: "We decry this overreaching by the government and assert again the inviolability of the right of human privacy." (The bishops were unwilling or unable to cite specific examples of this coercion. In fact, on the state level, a few existed, in violation of federal law. North Carolina, for a few years, required welfare recipients to take instructions in the use of birth control devices; the Department of Health, Education and Welfare ordered this practice halted in 1968.)

A few militant black leaders shared the bishops' point of view. In August 1968, for example, William Haden, a black activist in the Homewood-Brushton section of Pittsburgh, and a black physician, Dr. Charles E. Greenlee, demanded that Planned Parenthood stop dispensing birth control devices and information in that neighborhood. Greenlee said, "There will never be such a program in Homewood-Brushton as long as I am around to prevent it," and accused Planned Parenthood of committing "black genocide."[8] Planned Parenthood immediately ceased its operations— whereupon a group of 70 black women pleaded for a return of the program. One of the women said of Greenlee, "He's only one person—and a man at that. And he can't speak for the women of Homewood. He just doesn't speak for us. Birth control is none of his business."[9] In 1969, after President Richard M. Nixon gave a speech on the necessity of family planning, Marvin Davis, the Florida field secretary for the National Association for the Advancement of Colored People, reacted bitterly. "I do not think the President's plan is in the best interests of the black people," he said. "Our women need to produce more babies, not less. Our problems are mainly economic ones, and until we comprise 30 to 35 percent of the population, we won't be able to really affect the power structure in this country."[10]

One wonders whether Davis knew how closely his rhetoric paralleled the party line in Nazi Germany, where Aryan women were to become baby machines for the greater glory of the race.

The 1966 statement of the National Conference of Catholic Bishops prompted the following reaction from William H. Draper, Jr., national chairman of the Population Crisis Committee: "Someday I would hope that the 'freedom from external coercion' which the bishops so properly espouse for the family, would also be applied by the Catholic Church itself, and that when Pope Paul VI finally decides the birth control issue, the question of whether to practice birth control as well as the methods to be used, would be left to the conscientious decision of each Catholic couple. Then, indeed, will freedom from external coercion have been achieved."[11]

As we have seen, this was not to be. But when Pope Paul VI finally issued *Humanae Vitae*, the reaction of many Catholics, both in the United States and Europe, was a shrug of the shoulders. Joseph Cunneen, editor of *Cross Currents*, an ecumenical journal founded by Catholics, said, "It's no longer a point of controversy or even interest in the American Catholic Community. The Catholic Community has enough faith to say that the Catholic Church was wrong on birth control, but apparently the Pope does not."[12] And the Swiss theologian the Reverend Dr. Hans Kung said the encyclical demonstrated not only that the pope was not infallible, but also that he was wrong. This refusal to adapt church teaching to reality, Kung warned, could constitute a new "Galileo Case."[13] (It would not be until 1980, 300 years after the fact, that the church would acknowledge that perhaps it had been a bit harsh in condemning Galileo for insisting, on the basis of scientific observation, that the Earth is not the center of the universe.)

The extent of the derision and indifference with which the encyclical was met seemed to surprise even the pope himself. In June 1969, nearly a year after it was issued, he accused his critics of trying to make life too easy: "We ask ourselves if, among the motives of objection raised with respect to the encyclical, there is not that of a secret thought: to abolish a difficult law to render life more easy." And the Vatican newspaper *L'Osservatore Romano* claimed that humanity should be grateful to the pope for continuing the ban on birth control, "which saves mankind from itself and from the dehumanizing effect of unbridled sexuality." (Was this not precisely the sentiment expressed by Dr. and Mrs. Jack C. Willke in their comparison of unrepressed sexuality with an alcoholic binge?)

In the United States, however, one faction strongly supported the pope, and that was the bishops. The office of Archbishop Terence J. Cooke of New York said the encyclical was "an authoritative teaching on the part of the Pope that does require assent by Catholics." James Francis Cardinal McIntyre of Los Angeles said it was "in conformity with time-established principles of right reason and scientific research." In the District of Columbia, Patrick Cardinal O'Boyle angered his parishioners by disciplining 44 priests who had written a "letter of conscience" in which they said birth control was a matter for the individual to decide. Two hundred people walked out of St. Matthew's Cathedral as O'Boyle read a statement which deplored the idea that free will might have a part to play in such matters: "My dear friends in Christ, can you understand that I am impelled to act because I cannot stand by and let you be misled by an idea of freedom of conscience that could bring down on you so horrible a curse?"

In their ongoing battle against artificial birth control, the conservatives who controlled the Catholic Church used the following arguments:

—Artificial birth control is inherently immoral.

—Artificial birth control encourages immoral behavior.

—Those who say artificial birth control is needed to control population are wrong; the term "population explosion" is an exaggeration, and more efficient methods of food production should result in the eradication of global starvation.

—Those who say artificial birth control is needed to control population are actually motivated by a desire to reduce or eliminate certain "undesirable" peoples.

—The availability of artificial birth control interferes with the "right" of all couples to have many children.

—The availability of artificial birth control will lead to the mandatory use of artificial birth control.

What is significant about these arguments is that in each case, the church eventually replaced the phrase "artificial birth control" with the word "abortion." By the end of the 1960s, the church, which had been the chief adversary of artificial birth control, began diverting some of its resources to a crusade against abortion. In this effort, the church picked up new allies. Usually these allies were Catholics; usually they were people who agreed with the church's stand on birth control, but had never felt the need to take action on it.

As we have seen, most American Catholics paid little attention to church leaders who told them to stay away from artificial birth control. Similarly, most Catholics came to disagree with their leaders about abortion—which is not to say that most Catholics favored abortion; they declared that abortion was a matter of personal choice, rather than public policy. Who, then, agrees with the church's assertion that abortion constitutes murder, and should be outlawed?

Let us answer that question by jumping to the summer of 1980, to the eighth annual convention of the National Right to Life Committee in Anaheim, California. It is June 27. Dr. Jack Willke of Cincinnati has just been elected to a one-year term as president of the organization, fulfilling an eight-year-old ambition. The same constituency that bought his books and applauded his lectures has now provided him with a power base from which he will soon have easy access to the President of the United States. In a meeting room off the lobby of the Anaheim Convention Center, Francis X. Maier, the editor of the *National Catholic Register*, is instructing right-to-life activists about dealing with the media. Maier says the issue is not just abortion, but a battle between two opposing philosophies of life. The first, he says, is secular humanism, which places Man at the center of the meaning of existence. Proabortionists adhere to this philosophy, he says. They are frequently Republicans. They have high incomes and small families, and tend to be well-educated professional people. "In other words," says Maier, "what we're dealing with ... is an economic and cultural elite who are accustomed to wielding power." (The media, Maier warns, are dominated by secular humanists.)

The other philosophy is the Judeo-Christian ethic. Right-to-lifers, he says, believe that man has a higher purpose than simple self-fulfillment. He characterizes right-to-lifers as middle- and lower-middle-class working people; family-oriented; blue collar. They are less mobile than those who favor legalized abortion. Their education is more modest. They are religious. And they tend to be Democrats.

Though oversimplified, Maier's analysis was essentially correct. The struggle over abortion is not primarily a religious struggle. It is a class struggle. In the minds of right-to-lifers, the enemy is what is perceived as the ruling elite—the Kennedys, the Rockefellers, the Fords. The right-to-lifers are the people unmoved by the sexual revolution, the people who shared the sentiments expressed in *How to Teach Your Children the Wonders of Sex*. They are conservative Catholics and fundamentalist Protestants.

CHAPTER 2

OF BISHOPS AND CONVERTS

Right-to-life leaders today stress the religious diversity of the movement. In the summer of 1980, for example, Jack C. Willke said of the National Right to Life Committee, "We are not in any remote sense of the word a religious organization. We have people of a bewildering variety of faiths and non-faiths." Yet one crusader who recently gained acclaim within the movement insists, to the consternation of many of her more cautious colleagues, that Catholicism is at the heart of right-to-life philosophy. Her name is Elasah Drogin. She is president of Catholics United for Life, an organization headquartered in a commune in the southern foothills of the Sierra Nevada in the town of Coarsegold, California. The six families that make up the commune live in a rambling one-story wooden building that appears to have grown randomly, rather than according to any particular design. The inside is rough and unfinished. Fiberglass insulation hangs from the walls and ceilings. But it is comfortable and roomy, and the children of the commune families scamper about happily. Elasah Drogin is the mother of seven of these children. She is tall and thin, with pale blue eyes and long straight brown hair.

She founded the commune specifically to fight abortion. In a 1980 leaflet entitled "Why I Am a *Catholic* Prolife Worker," she wrote:

> The prolife movement has been a failure up till now, for more babies than ever are going to the crematoriums today which are thousands of times more effective than Hitler's. That is why we advocate that Catholic families band together in communities for the purpose of mutual support so that we can live a truly Catholic life and avoid paying income taxes which the government uses for abortion and sterilization programs throughout the world.
>
> This certainly is a Catholic issue because of the fact that the innocent victims *are not baptized.* Only Catholics believe these babies are cheated out of life *and heaven.*
>
> If Catholics were to pull out of the prolife movement it would instantly and completely die out. Abortion is most certainly a Catholic issue—and when we say it is not, we are only confusing the issue; we want these babies to have the opportunity to choose baptism. Baptism is more important to us than physical life. That is why the vast majority of prolife workers are Catholic. To be ashamed of it is to be counterproductive.

Elasah Drogin takes a hard line against abortionists. "Please help us talk people out of supporting these murderers," she wrote, "for I promise you that, even if abortion is made illegal tomorrow, key abortion figures will someday be hunted down like Nazi war criminals and brought to justice for crimes against humanity." It has been a long and curious journey for this woman who grew up in the Midwest, rich, liberal—and Jewish.

The early months of 1968 were heady times for anti-war activists in the United States. A Minnesota senator named Eugene McCarthy was seriously challenging President Lyndon B. Johnson; as the primary season approached, it actually seemed possible that McCarthy might succeed in toppling the President. At the University of California at Berkeley, where student protests against the war had begun, those in the movement could sense that the hated establishment was beginning to lose its grip.

But for one of the Berkeley activists, the excitement of the political ferment—along with every other aspect of her life—suddenly receded into the pale gray background. In the foreground was a single assumption, an ugly blotch suddenly thrust between her and her vision of the future: she thought she was pregnant. And she knew, with no less certainty than if she had discovered a malignant tumor within her, that she had to get rid of this thing.

Her name was Elasah Engel then. She was from Ohio, from a wealthy Jewish family. She was twenty-one years old. She was not married, and had no intention of getting married. She did not tell the man with whom she had slept of her probable condition. The problem resided within her, not him.

When she missed her first menstrual period, she went to the office of an organization called the Association for the Repeal of Abortion Laws. She was given a pregnancy test, with negative results. She was told to come back for a second test if she missed another period. She did, and this time the test was positive. She thought to herself, very clearly, "I don't want this baby."

A friend of her brother drove her south, through Los

Angeles, through San Diego, across the Mexican border. For a while they drove through slums, and then suddenly they entered a wealthy neighborhood. They found the address they had been given and stopped in front of a house. There was an operating room in the house. A man who was holding a drink gestured for Elasah to go in. She was frightened. Yet she was determined to go through with the abortion anyway, even with her own health at risk. She wanted desperately to get rid of the being that had intruded on her life. She was given a general anesthetic.

When she awakened, she was in another room. The man who had performed the abortion—she never did find out whether or not he was a doctor—was there with her. He was *angry* with her. "Your body kept fighting against me," he told her. "You kept trying to close your cervix. I had to give you more anesthetic." And he told her that her fetus—her baby, he called it—"had bones."

Elasah Engel was one of perhaps 10 million women desperate enough to seek out illegal abortions during the 1960s. Estimates—none particularly reliable—ranged from 200,000 to two million a year. (The low figure is almost certainly wrong, since experts in New York and California regularly put the number of abortions in each of those states at 100,000 a year. And a University of Colorado study done in the late fifties concluded that "postoperative complications" resulted from 350,000 illegal abortions a year—making the actual number of abortions much higher.) Occasionally these illegal abortions were performed under safe and humane conditions. For perhaps 40 years Dr. Robert Douglas Spencer, of Ashland, Pennsylvania, performed antiseptic abortions for $100 or less. On east coast campuses, Dr. Spencer, an atheist, acquired the nickname "The Angel of Ashland." In 1956 one of his patients died of a freak reaction to sodium pentothol while he was performing an abortion on her. He was arrested and charged with performing an illegal abortion. At his trial, he admitted as much. A jury of seven men and five women deliberated for four hours, then declared Spencer not guilty. Asked how this was possible, a town official remarked, "There aren't too many people in this county he hasn't helped."[1] Further west, eight or nine women a week found their way to the home of an elderly widow, LaVagne Michael, just a few blocks from the county courthouse in Rapid City, South Dakota. Mrs. Michael was a popular woman in Rapid City. Her son was a prominent optometrist and her daughter was married to a city councilman. She had been performing abortions since 1932. In 1962 Rapid City named her Gold Star Mother of the Year; a few weeks later she was arrested for performing an illegal abortion. She pleaded guilty, much to the relief of the district attorney, who wondered where he would find an impartial jury for her. She was sentenced to three years' probation.[2]

But most women, particularly poor women, were not fortunate enough to find a Douglas Spencer or a LaVagne Michael. The experiences they underwent while attempting to end their pregnancies were usually harrowing, often injurious, and sometimes fatal. It is worth quoting at length from a physician who witnessed the results of abortions botched by amateurs and quacks. Dr. Bernard Nathanson was a resident obstetrician-gynecologist at Women's Hospital in Manhattan, near Harlem, during the late fifties and throughout the sixties. In his book *Aborting America*

Nathanson described a routine shift at the hospital:

> During a typical thirty-six-hour "on call" shift I would
> be informed at 2 A.M. or thereabouts that a clinic pa-
> tient was bleeding in the Emergency Room. I would
> haul myself out of bed, struggle into my whites and
> trudge down to the E.R. There a petrified, shivering
> creature would be lying on the examining table, bleeding
> profusely from the vagina, and moaning softly to herself.
> Invariably, the patient would be black or Puerto Rican.
> A thermometer registering 103 or 104 would be taken
> from her mouth and with this, the moaning would give
> way to loud cries or praying in tongues. Skipping intro-
> ductions or interrogations, I would proceed immediately
> to the ordeal of vaginal examination, often fishing out
> sizable chunks of pregnancy tissue lying free among the
> huge clots. Another victim of a hack abortionist or of
> self-abortion. I would sign the admission slip, ordering
> intravenous antibiotics, blood tests, and preparations for
> a dilation and curettage (D and C). I would pass an hour
> or two mindlessly watching the "Late Late Show" on
> the dilapidated TV set in the residents' quarters until it
> was time to carry out the D and C, removing the rest of
> the tissue. If she were lucky, she would be returned to
> her room, be discharged forty-eight hours later, and in-
> structed to return to the gynecology clinic one month
> hence.
>   If she were *not* lucky, she might:
>   —Vomit under anesthesia, aspirate her vomitus, and
> die of respiratory obstruction and cardiac arrest.
>   —Continue to bleed from a perforation of the uterus
> that had been inflicted by the abortionist. Hysterectomy
> (removal of the uterus, causing lifelong sterility) would
> be carried out without delay.
>   —Continue to spike high fevers for days or weeks. In
> that era we had only a few antibiotics available, and most

had serious side effects. This might culminate in the formation of multiple pelvic abscesses, requiring periodic drainage of the pus which would collect. The pus was usually fulvous, wrenchingly foul-smelling, and so astonishing in quantity that even those hardened to it had to marvel at the body's ability to tolerate such pervasive corruption. In many cases the infection would be uncontrollable by means short of hysterectomy.

—Occasionally, even a hysterectomy would not slow the steady march of internal gangrene, and the woman would die painfully, her vital organs filthy with the satellite abscesses of her disease.

The passage quoted above is extraordinary, partially because, by 1980, its author had become a prominent right-to-lifer. After years of fighting to legalize abortion, and after performing or supervising thousands of abortions, he gradually switched sides; strangely, like Elasah Drogin, he now favors a restoration of the conditions that regularly resulted in the tragedies he so convincingly described.

Until 1967, laws in all 50 states prohibited abortions in all but the most dire circumstances—usually, only when the life of the mother was seriously threatened by the pregnancy. Efforts to reform these laws began in 1959, when the American Law Institute proposed permitting abortions under the following circumstances:

—If the continuation of the pregnancy would gravely impair the physical or mental health of the mother.

—If the doctor believed that the child would be born with a grave physical or mental defect.

—If the pregnancy had resulted from either rape or incest.

To guard against abuse of the law, the American Law

Institute recommended that two physicians certify in writing that at least one of these conditions existed.

The following year, the American Medical Association called for reform under essentially the same guidelines, adding that abortions should be allowed in the cases of very young or mentally incompetent girls. The men who authored the AMA report, Dr. James M. Kummer, a psychiatrist at UCLA, and Zad Leavy, a deputy district attorney for Los Angeles County, said that one out of every five pregnancies in the United States ended in an illegal abortion.

In 1962, a woman named Sherri Finkbine sought an abortion. Mrs. Finkbine was hostess of a local television show in Phoenix, Arizona. She was married and had four children. Early in her fifth pregnancy, she took a drug called thalidomide. She then discovered that in Europe, where thalidomide had been widely prescribed, thousands of severe birth defects had resulted. Children were born stunted, retarded, without arms and legs. Mrs. Finkbine was unable to obtain an abortion in the United States. Eventually she went to Sweden, where doctors performed an abortion and confirmed that the fetus was severely deformed. The wide media coverage of the Finkbine case spurred reform efforts in the United States.

In 1963 and '64, an epidemic of rubella (German measles) swept through the United States. Rubella is usually a mild disease that lasts from a few days to two weeks and has no lasting effects. But the results of rubella in women during early pregnancy are often devastating. During the course of the epidemic, 20,000 women who had contracted rubella delivered stillborn babies. Another

30,000 had babies with severe mental or physical defects.

During this period the number of prestigious groups calling for reform of abortion laws in America grew steadily. In 1962 the United Presbyterian Church became the first major religious organization to urge uniform laws for therapeutic abortions. In 1963 the American Lutheran Church Executive Committee and the Unitarian Universalist Association joined in, and in 1964 the International Congress on Penal Law concurred.

In 1966, a reform bill was introduced in the New York State House of Representatives. It would have permitted abortions when the mother's health was threatened, or when it appeared likely that the child would be born with severe defects, or when the pregnancy resulted from rape or incest. Harriet Pilpel, a lawyer for the American Civil Liberties Union, estimated that the 100,000 abortions taking place in New York State each year were not all strictly illegal. Pilpel said, "The New York Statute, which, to quote its language, permits abortion only when 'necessary to preserve the life of the woman or of the child,' is similar to the law in most other states. In interpreting these statutes, many cases hold that the threat to life need not be 'imminent' or 'certain.'"[3]

The New York bill was defeated in 1966, and reintroduced in 1967. As had been the case with artificial birth control, the primary opposition came from the Roman Catholic hierarchy. In February 1967, the bishops of New York State did something they had never done—they issued a joint pastoral letter, to be read in all dioceses in the state. In it, they urged all Catholics to fight the reform law. "Since the laws which allow abortion violate the unborn child's God-given right, we are opposed to any proposal to extend them. We urge you most strongly to do all in your power to prevent direct attacks on the lives of unborn children."

Meanwhile, in Connecticut—a predominantly Roman Catholic state—a more limited reform bill was introduced. It would have permitted abortions for victims of rape and for girls under the age of sixteen. The three bishops of Connecticut issued a statement deploring the bill: "However convenient, convincing, or compelling the arguments in favor of abortion may be, the fact remains that the taking of a life, even though it is unborn, cuts the very heart out of the principle that no one's life, however unwanted or useless it may be, may be terminated in order to promote the health or happiness of another human being."[4]

The sort of language employed by the bishops of Connecticut and New York was offensive to many people, including religious leaders of other faiths, who realized quickly that the bishops were accusing them of condoning murder. On February 24, 1967, the Protestant Council of New York City, along with three Jewish organizations, issued the following understatement:

"We do not feel, for example, that the case of ecumenism is best served by attributing to us the advocacy of murder and genocide." The clergymen added that those who share concern for human life may sincerely differ on the point at which human life begins, and "the conditions under which it is theologically or socially allowable to end it."[5]

(By this time, opponents of abortion reform were in the habit of comparing the reformers to Nazis. In the ongoing New York debate, for example, Assemblyman John H. Terry, a Syracuse Republican, compared the abortions of defective fetuses with the elimination of "defective Jewish persons" during the Third Reich.)[6]

The campaign of the Catholic hierarchy against abortion reform officially became nationwide on April 13, 1967. On that day the National Conference of Catholic Bishops, which only six months earlier had accused the Johnson Administration of coercion in the area of artificial birth control, launched an all-out attack on abortion. The NCCB budgeted $50,000 to begin a campaign to educate Catholics and non-Catholics alike. The action was proposed by one of the Connecticut bishops, the Most Reverend Walter W. Curtis of Bridgeport, who announced with alarm that the number of states in which there were campaigns to liberalize the abortion laws had jumped from 12 to 31 within a year. Curtis said the church's Family Life Bureau, which would run the program, would "underscore the teaching of the church." He emphasized that it would not become involved in political action. "That," he said, "is essentially the task of our citizens."

It was in 1967, however, that reformers made the first dents in the solid wall of antiabortion laws that had been in place for a century. On April 25, the first successful abortion reform bill in the nation was signed into law—not in New York, but in Colorado. The bill was based on the model proposed by the American Law Institute. It permitted abortions if the fetus was likely to have grave or permanent mental or physical damage; if the pregnancy had occurred through rape, incest, or statutory rape; or if the mother risked grave mental or physical harm in carrying on the pregnancy. As a safeguard, three physicians were required to confirm in writing that at least one of these conditions pertained. The bill did not restrict abortions to residents of Colorado, which prompted Dr. Robert Stewart, a former president of the Catholic Physicians Guild, to complain, "The whole world now finds Colorado available."[7] (In fact, very few women found Colorado "available." During the first fourteen months the law was in effect, only 338 legal abortions were performed. Of these, 100 were done on women from outside the state. In addition to the strict requirements, there was the matter of price; legal abortions were unavailable for less than $500. In 1969 Dr. Harvey Cohen of Denver, who performed many of the abortions, called the law "a noble experiment in social justice that failed." He added, "This is a rich lady's law."[8])

In May 1967, North Carolina enacted a bill similar to Colorado's—except that abortions there were restricted to women who had been residents of the state for at least four months. This was North Carolina's way of avoiding the title "Abortion Capital of the United States."

A month later, the governor of California signed into law an abortion reform bill. His name was Ronald Reagan, and it was not something he wanted to do.

Under California's 1872 law, abortion was legal only to save the life of the mother. The first reform bill was introduced in 1962, only to die in committee. But the rubella epidemic of 1963 and '64 gave impetus to the reform movement. By 1965, some California doctors were openly admitting that they performed abortions for reasons not countenanced by the law—particularly in cases where the fetus was likely to be defective. Local newspapers took note of this. The publicity particularly annoyed one highly placed Catholic obstetrician, Dr. James V. McNulty of Los Angeles, a member of the state's Board of Medical Examiners. "We took an oath to uphold the law," McNulty warned the board. "These doctors who admit doing abortions for rubella are saying they're above the law. If we don't punish them, we're guilty of malfeasance."[9]

McNulty's remarks triggered a crackdown. Many hospitals that had been tolerant of abortions for women who had contracted German measles in early pregnancy now put a stop to the practice. But the crackdown angered many doctors—so much so that they organized to support the reform bill sponsored by State Senator Anthony C. Beilenson of Beverly Hills. It is likely that McNulty's crackdown provided the impetus that eventually carried the reform measure into law.

California in 1967 was 25 percent Catholic. The church leadership immediately mobilized to fight the Beilenson bill. The Diocese of Los Angeles, under the leadership of the archconservative James Francis Cardinal McIntyre, set up a Right to Life League, featuring a bureau of speakers who would go anywhere in the state to deliver the anti-abortion line. They were supplemented by a group of Catholic women who called themselves MOMI (Mothers Outraged at Murder of Innocents). The diocese also hired a public relations firm, Spencer-Roberts Associates, to fight for the maintenance of the old law. One of Spencer-Roberts's other clients was the governor, Ronald Reagan. Cardinal McIntyre personally phoned Reagan and asked him to fight the bill. The governor said he would.

Nevertheless, the bill cleared the Senate Judiciary Committee. At this stage it would have permitted abortions under three conditions: if the pregnancy were likely to gravely impair the physical or mental health of the mother; if the pregnancy were the result of rape or incest; or if the fetus were likely to be physically or mentally defective Governor Reagan announced that if the bill cleared both houses in this form he would veto it because of this final provision. "A crippled child has a right to live," he said, and complained that the idea of aborting defective fetuses was "only a step away from what Hitler tried to do."

Because of the rubella scare, the provision about defective fetuses was the one most avidly sought by reformers. But, in order to save the rest of the bill, Senator Beilenson removed it. The bill passed. Governor Reagan—whose only public objection to the measure had been corrected—had no choice but to sign it. His political error had been to limit his criticism to one section of the bill; his philosophical error, in right-to-life terms, had been to confine the Nazi analogy to only one aspect of the abortion issue. His logic was inconsistent; if an innocent deformed fetus deserved protection, then why not a fetus, no less innocent, created through an act of rape or incest? And why not a fetus which, through no fault of its own, might cause physical or mental harm to its mother? Reagan apparently realized this inconsistency, and later repudiated it by renouncing the abortion measure he had signed into law.

It is probable that Ronald Reagan's distaste for abortion reform also stemmed from an aspect of morality that has nothing to do with the alleged killing of babies: the issue of sex between unmarried persons, particularly teenagers. Reagan was against it. In 1969, a gonorrhea epidemic of massive proportions was sweeping California. Some 250,000 cases were treated that year—half in persons under the age of twenty-five. In an effort to gain some control of the disease, the California House and Senate passed a bill striking down a law that prohibited the sale of prophylactics to minors. Governor Reagan vetoed the bill. "The moral issues inherent in this bill," he said, "must outweigh whatever medical advantages which might result from its approval." Did Reagan believe his veto would prevent teenagers from having sex? This seems unlikely, in view of the venereal disease rate, which indicated conclusively that, prophylactics or not, a high percentage of California teenagers was far from chaste. While Reagan may have thought that his veto would act as a deterrent to some teenagers, there was also a punitive aspect to his action. He seemed to be saying, "If you're going to have sex, you're going to have to pay the price." This line of reasoning is strong in both anti-birth control and antiabortion thinking. (In 1970, the Legislature again approved the sale of prophylactics to minors; this time, faced with a gonorrhea rate that had increased still further, Reagan allowed the bill to become law.)

In signing the abortion reform bill, Reagan was acknowledging that a fetus is not entitled to the same rights as its mother. Some right-to-lifers—most significantly Ellen McCormack, the Long Island housewife who ran for president in 1976 and again in 1980—would never forgive him.

But California did not become the abortion capital of the United States. The new law was cumbersome. Doctors were reluctant to test its boundaries. Women seeking abortions had to overcome a series of obstacles in order to reach their goal. Most used the justification of mental health; these needed referrals from their own doctors and written permission from a second obstetrician-gynecologist and a psychiatrist. The information in these documents was then reviewed by a hospital committee, often arbitrarily formed. Doctors' fees and hospital charges often amounted to $600 for an early abortion. Thus, it was another "rich lady's law." During the first half of 1968, 2,035 legal abortions were performed in California—while an additional 50,000 *illegal* abortions took place. Some California residents, like Elasah Engel, crossed over into Mexico for their abortions.

Engel's abortion was relatively sanitary and painless. It was performed in a clean house, in a clean room, by someone who had the technical skill to do it (there were no postoperative physical complications). But the doctor— if he was a doctor—clearly lacked a bedside manner. Perhaps it was the manner in which he scolded her when she awakened; perhaps it was what he told her about the fetus's bones. Whatever it was, it combined with something deep in her psyche to cause her to lapse into a depression, and then to set off on a spiritual journey that eventually resulted in her dedicating her life to making abortion illegal for all time. During the next two years she felt worthless. Her life seemed as cheap as the life of the baby she had surrendered. While she was not particularly suicidal, she felt that she would not live for more than two years.

She began reading the Bible. The Old Testament revealed to her the possibility that Jesus Christ could be the Messiah. Soon she converted to Christianity, and then to

Catholicism (she now calls herself "a completed Jew"). The Catholic Church, she thought, had always, *always* been against abortion. Abortion, she discovered, was destroying society. It made life cheap. It revealed a lack of caring "for ourselves and for our children." And it relieved men of the responsibility of taking care of the children they had fathered. She married, and began to have children. What she had done in Mexico, she had decided, had been purely for *convenience*. The absolute desperation to get rid of that fetus—the willingness to go through with an operation at the hands of someone with dubious credentials and a drink in his hand, the determination to rid herself of this thing or die trying—all of this, she later decided, had resulted from a desire not to be inconvenienced.

While Elasah Engel became Elasah Drogin and formulated her antiabortion philosophy, the abortion reform movement in the United States continued to make steady progress. In 1968 a presidential advisory council headed by former Senator Maurine Neuberger of Oregon recommended the revocation of all laws making abortion a crime. (The commission, which had been established to suggest ways of improving the status of women, also recommended that full legal rights be granted to illegitimate children, and that women should be given the right to establish their own domiciles, for whatever purpose. At the time, women had this right in only six states.) International Planned Parenthood and its affiliate, the World Population Council, for the first time advocated the widespread use of abortion. In 1969 the National Association for the Repeal of Abortion Laws was founded, and by the end of the year, reform laws similar to those in California and Colorado had been

passed in eight other states. A court decision also added to
the momentum. In the District of Columbia, Judge Gerhard
Gesell ruled that a law there prohibiting abortion except
when a pregnant woman's life or health was in danger was
unconstitutionally vague, and interfered with doctor-
patient privacy. The result of this decision was to leave the
nation's capital with no abortion statutes whatsoever.

Still, by the end of 1969, fewer than 14,000 legal
abortions were being performed annually in the United
States—about three quarters of them in California. Meanwhile, according to the best estimates, the number of illegal abortions remained at one million annually. Thus, for
every woman able to obtain a legal abortion, another 71
women were forced to take their chances with those working outside the law.

But during the last six months of 1970, all of that
would begin to change. And the change would commence
in the State of New York.

CHAPTER 3

NEW YORK – ABORTION CAPITAL OF THE NATION

The apotheosis of Dr. Bernard Nathanson, the abortionist turned right-to-lifer, reached its peak at the National Right to Life Committee Convention in Anaheim, California, on the evening of June 26, 1980. There, he stood on a stage and told of his sins as a master abortionist to more than a thousand delegates. As director of the Center for Reproductive and Sexual Health in New York City from early 1971 to late 1972, he had supervised the deaths of tens of thousands of innocent unborn babies, he said. With a certain bravado he confessed, "It was not just *an* abortion clinic, but *the* abortion clinic." There were gasps in the audience when he told of the scurrilous role of the clergy in the abortion business: "curiously, ladies and gentlemen, it was established and fed by the Clergy Consultation Service, an organization of 1200 Protestant ministers and Jewish rabbis who took it upon themselves to funnel through *60,000* young women in the space of the 19 months I ran it."

The audience nodded knowingly as Nathanson described the tactics he and the other members of the National Association for the Repeal of Abortion Laws used to con the State of New York into legalizing abortion. "We fed them a line of deceit, of dishonesty, of fabrication of statistics, figures; we coddled and caressed—stroked—the press; we cadged money from various sources, and we, in one short year, succeeded in striking down the abortion laws in New York State. And in one fell swoop we established the City of New York as the abortion capital of the world."

At the end of the speech, most of the audience applauded wildly. Many of the delegates bought copies of Nathanson's book, *Aborting America*, which was available at the back of the hall, and brought these up to the stage to be autographed. Surely Nathanson was one of them now. Earlier, when outgoing National Right to Life Committee President Dr. Carolyn Gerster had introduced him, she read the inscription he had written in *her* copy of his book: "'Best of luck in your...no, *our*...movement.'" If Dr. Nathanson had performed thousands of abortions—what of it? As the delegates frequently said to one another, he had come so far!

Indeed he had. On Sunday, June 28, 1970—ten years earlier, almost to the day—the *New York Times Magazine* carried an article heralding the advent of legalized abortion on demand, which was to go into effect three days later. Accompanying the article was a photograph of an earnest young doctor wearing a laboratory coat. He was broad-faced, serious, with dark hair, olive skin, and a wide, intelligent mouth. He wore dark-framed glasses. He smiled pleasantly. He held a suction tube which was attached to a jar in the foreground. The caption said, "Dr. Bernard Nathanson, chief of gynecology at the Hospital for Joint Diseases, demonstrates a device for performing abortions by suction. He will preside July 1 at a training session on out-of-hospital abortions. The meeting, at N.Y.U., will be attended by 350 doctors." (In fact, Nathanson later recalled in his book, only 80 doctors showed up.)

In the *New York Times Magazine* article, Nathanson was quoted as follows:

> The word "abortion" still has a seriously soiled, stained meaning. People talk about New York becoming the abortion capital of the world as if that would be a terrible thing. But substitute 'heart transplant'—make New York the heart transplant capital of the world and see how their expressions change. Well, I don't think there should be a difference. I'd be proud if New York were humane enough and had enough compassion to become the abortion capital of the world, and I think we have to do everything in our power to make it possible.

Although legislation to liberalize New York's abortion laws had been introduced as early as 1966, the effort did not gain serious momentum until two years later, when Governor Nelson Rockefeller appointed an 11-member commission to study the question. The governor favored liberalization of the law, which permitted abortion only when the life of the mother was deemed to be in danger. The commission was dominated by people who shared that view. From the point of view of the antiabortionists, these included two particularly notorious men: Dr. Christopher Tietze of the National Population Council, a biostatistician who favored abortion as a means of curbing population growth, and Dr. Alan Guttmacher, president of the Planned Parenthood Federation of America.

The commission completed its work late in March 1968. The majority cited differences among ancient, as well as modern, theologians about when the fetus receives a soul, and said the premise that the fetus is "at all times a human being, possessed of corresponding legal rights . . . is clearly fallacious." The commission stopped short of recommending abortion on demand, but did advocate abortion under seven conditions:

—When the mother's physical or mental health would be gravely impaired by the pregnancy;

—When the fetus was likely to be severely mentally or physically deficient;

—When the woman was mentally or physically disabled to the point where she would be unable to care for the child;

—When the pregnancy resulted from rape;

—When the pregnancy resulted from incest;

—When the woman was unmarried and under the age of sixteen when she became pregnant, and was still unmarried;

—When requested by any woman who already had at least four children.

This last condition, of course, amounted to abortion on demand for mothers of four or more children; it was further than Governor Rockefeller had wished to go. He endorsed the first six conditions, but not the last.

Three members of the commission filed a minority report that opposed any liberalization whatsoever. They said the recommendations of the majority would violate "fundamental human rights of the human child." They also argued that widespread abortion would be "detrimental to

our traditional and still viable ideals of the sanctity of
innocent human life and the integrity of the family unit"—a
contention that would gain wide currency a few years later.
The three commissioners supporting the minority view
were Dr. John Grant Harrison, former president of the
Catholic Physicians Guild of New York State; Monsignor
William F. McManus, director of the Family Life Bureau of
the Archdiocese of New York, and Robert M. Byrn, associate professor of criminal law at Fordham University Law
School.

In 1968, for the third consecutive year, a bill to liberalize New York's abortion law was introduced, and for the
third consecutive year it was defeated. In 1969 the bill was
introduced again, and defeated again, although by a much
smaller margin. Neither of these bills would have legalized
anything approaching abortion on demand; both were similar to the measure passed in Colorado in 1967. How was
it, then, that a far more sweeping measure—one that allowed
abortion on demand up to the twenty-fourth week of
pregnancy—was approved in 1970? The answer lies in a
failed gamble by the antiabortion forces.

Earl Brydges, the majority leader in the New York
State Senate, opposed any liberalization of the New York
law. Brydges was extremely concerned by the increasing
support he saw for reform. So he put into effect a plan
which, he thought, would mobilize the broadest possible
opposition to the reform movement: he introduced what
he considered an outrageously permissive bill, one that
would make abortion a matter to be decided between a
woman and her doctor up to the twenty-fourth week of
pregnancy. Brydges, of course, opposed his own bill. But

he miscalculated. The Senate passed the bill and sent it on to the Assembly.

It was apparent to everyone that the vote in the Assembly would be close. Each member of the Assembly had been under pressure from both sides, and many had agonized over the vote. One in particular, George M. Michaels, who represented the predominantly Catholic area of Auburn, had not been able to find refuge from the abortion issue anywhere—not even within his own household. His wife and daughter argued that he should support the reform; Michaels resisted.

On April 9, the Assembly voted. George Michaels voted no. And when the roll was completed, the reform bill fell one vote short of passage.

Michaels stood and was recognized. "I realize, Mr. Speaker, that I am terminating my political career, but I cannot in good conscience sit here and allow my vote to be the one that defeats this bill." He changed his vote to "yes."

Speaking for the bishops of New York State, Terence Cardinal Cooke of New York City appealed to Governor Rockefeller to veto the bill, but Rockefeller signed it into law. On July 1, 1970, abortion on demand became a reality in New York.

In fact, during the next 30 months, New York State, and more specifically New York City, did become the abortion capital of the nation. Within the first six months, 69,000 legal abortions were performed in the city—half on women from outside the state. Manhattan became a mecca for women saddled with unwanted pregnancies, particularly college women. On at least two campuses—the

University of Maine and the University of Rhode Island—
student governments set up loan funds to help finance
trips to New York for abortions. Nine months after the
law had gone into effect, the number of legal abortions
passed 100,000, and the rate was 15,000 a month, and
climbing. Abortions were available in private hospitals for
as much as $650, and in clinics for as little as $80. The
Clergy Consultation Service, operating in more than 20
states, routinely referred women seeking abortions to the
clinics and hospitals of New York City. This referral service was free; others were not. The classified sections of
major newspapers throughout the country carried dozens
of ads each day: "Pregnant? Need Help?" "Where to get a
Safe, Legal ABORTION in New York"; "Abortion Counseling, Information, and Referral Service." Some of these
agencies were legitimate. Others would charge outrageous
fees for information available free elsewhere. (The referral
profiteers became so prolific that early in 1971 Planned
Parenthood of New York took out an ad in the *New York
Times* warning women against patronizing them.) In February 1971, Dr. Bernard Nathanson was named director
of the Center for Reproductive and Sexual Health, probably
the busiest abortion clinic in the world.

While all this was happening, the right-to-life movement
in New York State was coalescing and gaining power. The
rapid maturation of the movement in New York in the
1960s presaged the same phenomenon that would happen
on the national level in the 1970s.

In the early days of New York's right-to-life movement,
in 1963, a young lawyer named Robert M. Byrn, alarmed
by the stirrings of abortion reform, founded an organization

called the Metropolitan Right to Life Committee. (Byrn, as
we have seen, was one of the three dissenters to the Rockefeller Commission report.) He was the son of Roman Catholic parents who, he said in a 1971 interview, were "religious, but by no means fanatics." He grew up in the
Bronx. His education was in parochial schools: Fordham
Prep, Fordham University, and Fordham Law School. He
was a Wall Street lawyer for four years before joining the
Law School faculty at Fordham in 1963. He shrugged off
his Catholicism as incidental and irrelevant—the issue of
abortion, he said, was secular, not religious. But his Metropolitan Right to Life Committee—which sounded as much
like an insurance company as an antiabortion organization
—had its office in the Madison Avenue headquarters of the
Archdiocese of New York.

Byrn's organization never became predominant among
New York State's many right-to-life groups, although Byrn
himself became the movement's foremost legal authority.
By 1970 there were between 50 and 70 local right-to-life
groups in the state, most of them loosely affiliated with
the New York State Right to Life Committee, which was
founded in 1965 by Edward Golden of Brunswick, a small
town not far from the state capital of Albany.

Golden, too, was Catholic, with a Catholic education:
Catholic Central High School and Holy Cross College. He
was married, with six children. Like Byrn, he was disturbed
by the early abortion reform efforts, particularly the
model legislation proposed by the American Law Institute.
While Golden denied that his organization had any formal
connection with the church, he acknowledged that, prior
to 1972, 95 percent of the members of the New York

Right to Life Committee were Catholic. (In 1972, he re-
vised the figure downward to 85 percent.) Golden's executive committee often held meetings in a local church. He
denied taking direction from the church, however, and indeed, during those early days, the policy of the New York
Right to Life Committee and the position of the church
differed strongly on one aspect of the abortion issue:
whether or not to condemn the intrauterine device. The
committee did not oppose contraception—"abortion takes
a life, contraception only prevents it," was the official
position. The church lumped the IUD with other birth
control devices, and condemned them all. Thus, in those
early days, the right-to-life movement had not yet refined
the concept of zygote-as-person. The Catholic Church, of
course, already had.

By the time abortion on demand was legalized in New
York State, the New York Right to Life Committee was
five years old. But although Golden and his colleagues lobbied against the new law, most of the formal opposition
came from the church. It was only after the law was passed,
over the objections of the church, that the committee became a power in state politics.

In 1970 certain New York public officials were targeted for defeat because of their position on the abortion
issue. (Not until 1978 did the practice of targeting public
officials for defeat on the basis of their stands on single
issues begin to receive widespread national attention. In
that year, right-to-life political action committees targeted,
and took credit for helping to defeat, Senators Dick Clark
of Iowa, Ed Brooke of Massachusetts, and Thomas McIntyre
of New Hampshire.) The first target, appropriately enough,

was George Michaels, the assemblyman whose vote enabled the reform legislation to become law, and who had predicted, correctly, that the vote would cost him his political life. Under pressure from the right-to-lifers, Democratic party leaders failed to endorse Michaels for re-election in 1970, although normally he was a heavy vote getter. A political novice named John Rossi defeated Michaels in the Democratic primary; Rossi acknowledged that his campaign, and his victory, resulted from Michaels's vote on the abortion bill. Michaels did receive the endorsement of the state's Liberal Party, but ran third in the general election. Ed Golden explained the right-to-life philosophy on political campaigns in words that would be echoed by other right-to-life strategists throughout the 1970s: "To our way of thinking, any legislator who doesn't respect human life and protect it at all stages and despite infirmities is unfit to sit as a representative, and we would look for a man [sic] to replace him, and it didn't matter to us whether he was a Democrat, Republican, or independent or how he voted on any other issues."

The right-to-lifers advocated—and still advocate—one exception to this principle. When a powerful pro-choice *incumbent* is up for election, it is acceptable and sometimes desirable to vote for the opponent—even if that opponent is also pro-choice. For example, in the general election of 1970, right-to-lifers on Long Island targeted Republican Assemblyman Vincent R. Balletta, Jr., of Port Washington. Balletta had voted for the reform bill, but his Democratic opponent, Irwin Landes, also favored the liberal new law. Nevertheless, the words "Abort Balletta" appeared on signs and posters around the town, and Landes won. In

August 1972, Eleanor Tenner, secretary of the state Right to Life Committee, was quoted in the *New York Times Magazine* as follows:

> We got together a group of women to picket him wherever he went on his campaign, telling everybody who came to hear him that Balletta was proabortion. We knew Landes was, too, and we didn't expect him to vote for life—he had made his commitment. What we wanted to do was get rid of the Republican legislator who had gotten fairly well up on the seniority ladder. At least Landes, as a freshman, wouldn't have as much of a voice in the Legislature. And it worked. We beat Balletta by 6000 votes and after two years of Landes, now the Republicans have put up a candidate (Clinton Martin, Jr.) who's pledged to vote against abortion. Sometimes you have to take a step backward to take two steps forward.

But some right-to-lifers in New York did more than simply oppose candidates who disagreed with their points of view. In 1969, a group of housewives on Long Island formed their own political party.

In New York, more than in any other state, minor political parties play an important part in the electoral process. The state's Liberal and Conservative parties traditionally have fought for third place—that is, the third highest vote getter, behind Democrats and Republicans. Often these minor parties have played the role of spoiler, and occasionally they elect a candidate to a major political office. In 1969, for example, New York City Mayor John V. Lindsay, running for a second term, was repudiated in the primary by his own Republican Party. Lindsay was nominated by the Liberals, however, and went on to win. In 1972, the Conservative Party's candidate for United States senator, James Buckley, won in a three-way race against Republican incumbent Charles Goodell and the Democratic challenger, Richard Ottinger.

In any event, one day late in 1969, Ellen McCormack, Mary Jane Tobin, and several other housewives were having a book discussion at the home of Diane Arrigan in Merrick, Long Island. Someone mentioned that she had seen a piece on the news about the possibility of legalizing abortion. Everyone agreed that this would be awful. They started talking. Soon the New York Right to Life Party was born.[1] Its symbol, naturally, was a baby in a womb. The party ran two candidates for office in 1970—Mrs. Marcia Pilsner, thirty-one, of Seaford, Long Island, for lieutenant governor, and Mrs. James Gilroy, thirty-four, of Merrick, for governor. They did not receive a significant number of votes, and the archenemy, Nelson Rockefeller, was re-elected governor. But during the next eight years the strength of the Right to Life Party in New York would increase dramatically, and two of the founders, Ellen McCormack and Mary Jane Tobin, would play major roles.

Meanwhile, the Catholic Church remained the most influential voice against abortion in the state. On December 5, 1970, the 30 bishops of New York issued a second joint pastoral letter, in which they reaffirmed their earlier warning that the church would disavow, by immediate excommunication, any Catholic "who deliberately procures abortion or helps someone else to do so." The letter was significant for its emphasis on the business aspects of legalized abortion; the fact that people were making money from it was particularly abhorrent to the bishops. Once abortion had been legalized, they wrote, "abortionists lost no time plying their death-dealing trade." They continued, "Each day they grew wealthier from the killing of unborn children—some of whom have been heard to cry as they were dropped into the surgical trash cans. They even advertise their monstrous commerce beyond the confines of the state, thus making New York the abortion capital of America."

It was, of course, within the rights of the bishops to say what they pleased. As far as the State of New York was concerned, Catholics were perfectly free to abide by the dictates of the church. On the other hand, as far as the church was concerned, Catholics were not at all free to avail themselves of all the rights provided by the state—but there was nothing new in that, and nothing wrong with it, either, since theoretically a Catholic was free to leave the church whenever he or she chose to do so.

But the following year—when the church began to intervene directly in the electoral process—questions were raised about precisely how far the church should go before it would bulldoze the wall of separation between church and state. In 1971 the opponents of New York's new abortion law launched a drive to repeal it. While Edward Golden and others in various right-to-life organizations did most of the actual lobbying in Albany, the church spearheaded the drive to put popular pressure on the legislators. On April 24, Terence Cardinal Cooke said in a letter read in all 407 parishes of the New York Archdiocese: "There are bills in Albany right now that would stop the slaughter of the innocent unborn. I suggest that you write, phone, telegraph,

and speak to the state's lawmakers and make your support
of life known to them in a very clear manner.

"Some say that Catholics should not speak on this
issue," the Cooke letter continued. "'Abortion is only a
social matter,' they claim. 'Religion should not enter into
it.' Such a position disenfranchises men of certain religious
convictions. It says in effect that certain citizens may not
have a voice in particular issues."

Cooke was wrong, of course; nobody was saying that
Catholics should not speak on the issue. People *were* saying that Catholics should stop trying to impose their own
morality on non-Catholic citizens of a secular state. The
distinction was, and still is, regularly lost on the Catholic
leadership.

The pressure exerted by the church did not stop with
simple lobbying. There were no elections for state office in
1971, but there were local elections, and in at least one of
these, the Catholic Church played a crucial role.

On Sunday, September 12, two days before the primary to pick candidates for municipal and county offices,
the Reverend Eugene Keane of Saint Joseph's Church in
Croton Falls slipped mimeographed copies of a letter
inside the regular weekly bulletin that was distributed to
the parishioners. The letter was headlined, "Special Primary Notice," and it urged Catholics to make their choices
on the basis of how the candidates stood on abortion,
which the letter described as "intrinsically evil." The letter
made specific reference to a race for a seat in the legislature
of Westchester County: "We call to the attention of our
parishioners, regardless of party affiliation, that one of the
contestants (the incumbent) is reported in the press to be

'the spearhead' of the effort to prevent any change in the
New York abortion law ... In such circumstances, we feel
it incumbent upon us to make these activities known to
you." Similar letters were distributed that morning in the
five other parishes of Westchester County.

The targeted incumbent was R. Bradley Boal, a Republican and a leading member of the County legislature.
Westchester was a heavily Republican area and Boal was
considered a heavy favorite for re-election. In the primary
he faced John Hicks-Beach, who had the endorsement of
the Conservative Party as well. The right-to-life movement
opposed Boal vehemently because he was a past president
of the Westchester County office of Planned Parenthood
and was chairman of a statewide group called Committee
for Legal Abortion. On primary day, he lost to Hicks-Beach
by 120 votes.

Had the Reverend Keane written the letter himself?
Well, he said, the "basic document" had been given to him
by "citizens"; he recalled that he "may have" modified it.
He described the letter as "only routine," and added, "If it
had a political effect, it was accidental."[2]

Given the variety of antiabortion activity at various
levels of the church, one might expect that all of the criticism of the church's role would come from the liberal end
of the political spectrum—that is, from those who favored
the new abortion law. But this was not precisely the case.
Only a year after the new law had gone into effect, voices
on the right were complaining that the church was not
doing *enough* to combat it.

On June 20, 1971, the National Wanderer Forum, a
gathering of conservative Catholics, discussed at length the

issues of birth control and abortion. Among other things, they came out against a child advocacy system, and against the use of tax dollars to fund contraception, abortion, and sterilization; such programs of population control, they said, would aid in establishing "secular humanism" as a religion, and would thus violate the Constitution. One speaker, Dr. Ever Curtis, of Worcester, Massachusetts, said proudly that she was the only Catholic physician in Worcester who refused to prescribe birth control pills. "Irate husbands are almost ready to chop me into pieces because I won't give their wives the pill," she said, to loud applause.

Another speaker, John J. Mulloy, a Philadelphia teacher and writer, accused the bishops of New York State of failing to oppose with sufficient vigor the state's abortion law. Mulloy said the bishops were after tax money to support parochial schools, and were reluctant to make too much fuss about abortion. It would have been better to sacrifice the schools and uphold the moral principles involved, he said.

These attacks by the right would not be the last ones against the church. Throughout the decade, the bishops would be accused of similar sorts of compromises; in 1980, one group would even file suit against all Catholic archdioceses in the United States—much to the horror of other right-to-life organizations.

Toward the end of 1971, the drive to repeal the New York law faded temporarily, but antiabortion activity on other fronts increased. On November 20, several thousand antiabortion demonstrators marched down Fifth Avenue from 86th to 60th Street, chanting "Abortion is murder!" They were greeted warmly by Cardinal Cooke on the steps

of St. Patrick's Cathedral. On the same day, feminists ral-
lied in Washington to support the repeal of all restrictive
abortion laws in the United States, while 250 right-to-lifers
presented the draft of a constitutional amendment outlawing abortion to a sympathetic legislator, Representative
Lawrence J. Hogan of Maryland. Early in December,
Forham University Law Professor Robert M. Byrn, the
founder of the Metropolitan Right to Life Committee,
sought, and was granted, guardianship of tens of thousands
of fetuses in New York City.

In court, Byrn said that New York's law permitting
abortion on demand violated the Fourteenth Amendment
to the United States Constitution, which declares that no
state shall "deprive any person of life, liberty or property
without due process of law." On December 3, Byrn was
formally appointed guardian of Infant Roe, a fictitious
fetus representing all fetuses between the fourth and twenty-
fourth weeks of gestation scheduled to be aborted in New
York hospitals. Then, as guardian, Byrn asked the court to
issue a temporary injunction against these abortions.

On January 6, 1972, State Supreme Court Justice
Francis X. Smith granted the injunction. At a news conference following the ruling, Byrn showed slides of intact and
mutilated fetuses, which he said had been "killed by abortions." The ruling prompted Nancy Stearns, a lawyer for
the Center for Constitutional Rights, to ask that Byrn put
up a $40,000 bond for each woman forced to have a child
through his intervention.

Abortions in New York City were never actually halted,
however. Judge Smith's injunction was stayed pending appeal, and a month later the New York State Appellate

Division in Brooklyn overturned his ruling.

It was now an election year, something which the right-to-lifers felt would make their job easier. There is evidence that Governor Rockefeller agreed: early in the year, he announced his intention to veto any repeal bill that might pass the House and Senate. In essence, he was telling legislators who favored the new law but might feel politically compelled to vote for repeal to go ahead; the veto would cover them.

Meanwhile, the New York State Right to Life Committee and the Catholic Church—in concert, if not in direct association—renewed the crusade for the repeal of the abortion-on-demand statute, not yet two years old. Debate over the repeal bill was set for May. Cardinal Cooke declared April 17 "Right to Life Sunday," and on that day, 10,000 people paraded down Fifth Avenue to protest the law. At 72nd Street and Central Park a rally was held; both the parade and rally were sponsored by the Knights of Columbus.

By this time, orthodox Jews were also speaking out against the New York law. On April 23, the Rabbinical Council of America, the largest organization of orthodox Jews in the country, called for repeal; the rabbis' statement said abortions had "already assumed epidemic proportions" in the state. (In fact, the number of New York women seeking abortions had changed hardly at all, if the constant estimates of 100,000 *illegal* abortions a year prior to the time the law took effect were correct. The New York State Health Department reported that 262,807 legal abortions were performed in New York during 1971—but 61 percent of these were on out-of-state women. The remaining 39 percent—102,495—were on New York women.)

On April 26, Rockefeller announced that he would support a bill to shorten from 24 to 16 weeks the period in which abortion on demand would be legal, but this compromise was not acceptable to either side.

Then in early May, a week before the repeal bill was to come to the floor of the Senate, the President of the United States interjected himself into the debate. In a letter to Cardinal Cooke, Richard Nixon said he agreed with the cardinal's stand on abortion. "This is a matter for state jurisdiction, outside federal jurisdiction," he wrote, but added, "I would personally like to associate myself with the convictions you deeply feel and eloquently express."

Cooke's office triumphantly released the letter to the press; a spokesman for Nixon said later it had been meant as a private communication.

The debate in the Legislature was unrestrained. In the Assembly, Neil W. Kelleher, a Troy Republican, displayed an aborted fetus in a jar and called New York "the nation's number one abortion mill." In the Senate, James H. Donovan distributed packets of photographs of aborted fetuses bearing the inscription "What the unborn would like every legislator to know." Senator Emmanuel Gold of Queens responded by passing out coathangers to symbolize the lengths to which desperate women will go when legal abortion is not available. The repeal bill passed both houses: 79-68 in the House, 30-27 in the Senate.

Now, only one man could prevent New York from returning to the days when abortion was legal only to save the life of the mother, and he did. In his veto message, Rockefeller specifically chastised the Catholic Church for its role in the debate: "I do not believe it right for one group to impose its vision of morality on an entire society." He added, "Neither is it just or practical for the state to dictate the innermost personal beliefs and conduct of its citizens." The message enraged many Catholics—who were further distressed when Cardinal Cooke invited Rockefeller to the annual Al Smith Dinner in the fall. Right-to-life groups issued a statement advising against "anyone of anti-abortion convictions appearing publicly with the governor."

Antiabortionists in New York would not get a chance to wage another repeal effort in 1973, because in January of that year the United States Supreme Court was to strike down all restrictive antiabortion laws in the country. By that time, though, the philosophical base for a *national* antiabortion effort was largely in place, thanks to the work of a few early theoreticians in other parts of the country.

CHAPTER 4

WORDS AND PICTURES

Father Paul Marx of Collegeville, Minnesota, is a rugged-looking, broad-shouldered man, round-faced, with a receding hairline and a broad grin. He speaks earnestly, with great intensity. By 1970, Marx, then fifty, had already been speaking out regularly against abortion for about eight years. He had also been speaking out against contraception, pornography, homosexuality, and sex education (as espoused by Planned Parenthood). At the time, his opposition to contraception was somewhat muted; he later acknowledged that "for propaganda reasons" he was not in the habit of publicly linking the evils of contraception with the ultimate evil, abortion. Yet he was coming to believe strongly that the two were inseparable, and that one inevitably led to the other. Father Marx had met Dr. and Mrs. Jack C. Willke from time to time in his travels, and the three had become friendly. They admired one another's accomplishments. And in the autumn of 1970, at a meeting of the California State Marriage Counselors Association, where the Willkes had come to lecture, they met again. Over lunch, Marx asked them if they were getting involved in right-to-life.

71

"What's that?" Jack Willke asked jokingly. The Willkes had not gotten involved in the abortion issue, although they had heard about it.

"Oh, you've got to get involved in that," said Paul Marx. "If we don't win the abortion thing the whole family might go down the tube."

Jack Willke looked at him and said seriously, "Paul, if we start getting involved in abortion, it'll swallow us up. We are absolutely up to here in sex education."

Paul Marx said, "Nothing else counts now but abortion."

Jack Willke still had no intention of getting involved, but to ease his conscience, once he was home in Cincinnati, he wrote a piece for a local paper in which he explained that, from a medical point of view, abortion is the killing of a human being. Then he prepared to return to his medical practice. But his piece in the paper was noticed.

Someone whom Barbara Willke still refers to as "this little housewife on the other side of town" called and said, "Dr. Willke, this abortion is *murder*, and you seem to know what it's about. We've got to do something!"

Willke answered that there was a need to get the word out over radio and television.

The little housewife from across town said, "Who will speak for us?"

Humbly, Dr. Willke said, "Well, I will," thinking that there might be one or two appearances and that would be the end of it.

The little housewife booked Willke on four programs in the next four weeks, fourteen in the following three months.

Meanwhile, the Willkes continued their sex education lectures—but now they were also beginning to include abortion in the discussion. In Pittsburgh one night, they talked with a nurse who gave antiabortion talks in the local high schools. The nurse asked the Willkes a question that may have had even more significance in their lives than Paul Marx's query about abortion. The nurse said:

"Are you using any *pictures?*"

The nurse added that in her own talks she used a series of photographs of developing fetuses which *Life* magazine had published in 1965. She said that people just don't seem to know how early the fetus begins to take on the physical characteristics we associate with human beings. People think they're dealing with a shapeless blob of protoplasm, when, in fact, they're not.

The Willkes thought pictures were a wonderful idea. But they concluded that showing photos of healthy, developing fetuses would tell only half the story. They needed something else—something that would drive home the horror of abortion in clear and unmistakable terms. And so they began collecting photos of aborted fetuses.

In early December 1970, they returned to Pittsburgh to give another talk. By this time, they had amassed enough pictures to put on display, and they unveiled these for the first time. The audience was impressed, convinced. ("Gosh, it went well," Barbara Willke recalls.) Pictures of torn and battered fetuses now became a permanent part of the Willkes' traveling gear.

At Christmastime, the Willkes decided to write a book about abortion. This they accomplished in four months. *Handbook on Abortion* is undoubtedly the best-selling

book in the right-to-life movement. In June 1980, it went
into its nineteenth printing. It has been published in Spanish, French, Malayan, Italian, Chinese, Portuguese, Swedish,
and "Spanish Latin American" editions. Jack Willke says
it has sold more than one million copies. It is written in
question-and-answer format, with the Willkes posing a
series of questions about various aspects of abortion, then
answering:

*Isn't it true that restrictive abortion laws are unfair to
the poor?*

It is probably true that it is easier for a rich person to
break almost any law, than for a poor person to do so.
Perhaps the poor cannot afford all the heroin they want.
Rich people probably can. Does that mean we should
make heroin available to everyone? Not everything
money can buy is necessarily good. The solution is not
to repeal laws, but to enforce them fairly. Laws restricting abortion can be, and frequently have been, ade-
quately enforced.

But it's still basically unfair, isn't it?

What is unfair is that poor people have not been given
an adequate education and an adequate opportunity to
better themselves. We will not eliminate poverty by killing poor people. The problem of the poor and the
under-educated is their destitution and their lack of
opportunity to achieve a better life, not the fact that
they have children. Some who live in ivory towers seem
unaware of this, but poor people themselves are very
much aware of it, as evidenced by the fact that they as
a group have cut their birth rate much less than middle
and upper class socio-economic groups.

But don't too many children add to the burden of their poverty?

Poverty is more than just a shortage of this world's goods. Poverty is also the lack of spiritual and cultural resources, and often accompanying it is despair, apathy, and helplessness. Those who lack material things, and often find their chances for improvement of their lot rather bleak, sometimes find that much of their personal fulfillment is the joy they find in their children.

Note that the Willkes do not provide direct answers to their own questions. Note also that the Willkes' statements are loaded with contradictions: the first answer in the above sequence concedes that poor people seek out abortions, while the second implies that abortions to poor women are the result of coercion, and amount to genocide ("We will not eliminate poverty by killing poor people"). The second statement also concedes that people with small families enjoy a higher standard of living than those with large families, while the third statement prescribes lots of children as a balm to the poverty-stricken. This lack of internal logic, however, has not been detrimental to sales; the one constant in the book, the premise that abortion is wrong, has been sufficient to make *Handbook on Abortion* an indispensable tool of activists in the movement.

As the Willkes were putting the finishing touches on their manuscript in April 1971, they realized that the final product would be more effective if it were to come complete with pictures. Their publisher agreed. They did not consider their own small collection adequate, so they commenced a frantic search, contacting friends from all

over the country and the world in an attempt to locate
graphic photographic evidence of the evil of abortion. Pictures poured in from a doctor in Maryland, another in
California, another in Canada. Hundreds of pictures of
bloody, battered, and dismembered fetuses, in color and
black and white. Enough, far more than enough for the
book; enough, in fact, for an excellent slide set. But that
would come later.

While the Willkes were plunging headlong into the
antiabortion business, Father Charles Fiore, another pro-
tége'of Father Paul Marx, was putting together a slide set
of his own—something that would not please Dr. Jack
C. Willke.

Father Charles Fiore was born and raised in Madison,
Wisconsin, the youngest of five children of immigrant
parents. After considering careers in journalism and the
law, he entered the Dominican order in 1954, and was or-
dained in 1961. By this time he had earned master's degrees in philosophy and theology, and he continued to lead
a scholarly life, teaching at Xavier University, at a black
school in New Orleans, and then at the College of St.
Thomas in Saint Paul, Minnesota. He also became an officer
in a voluntary association of Dominican priests, nuns, and
brothers called the Dominican Educational Association of
the United States; almost all of the members were involved
in some aspect of education. It was at a board meeting of
this group in the spring of 1967 that Fiore first thought
seriously about getting involved in the abortion issue.

This particular meeting was one of a series in which the
board discussed the social upheavals of the sixties and their
apparent effects on family life in the United States. They

talked about the birth control pill and the Vietnam war; in addition, there was a great deal of discussion about the turmoil within the Catholic Church itself. Fiore and his colleagues knew that there was a corollary to the old axiom "It's an ill wind that blows no good": it is also an unusual wind that blows no ill. In convening Vatican II, Pope John XXIII had made a remark about opening up the windows of the church to let in some fresh air, but many Catholics, including Fiore and his colleagues, concluded that while a lot of needed fresh air had come into the church, so also had a lot of dust and noise and grime. Not everything blowing in the wind was the Holy Spirit.

In the spring of 1967, abortion was in the news. Colorado was in the process of becoming the first state to liberalize its antiquated laws. There were also debates in California, North Carolina, and New York. Against this background, the Board of Directors of the Dominican Educational Association of the United States began talking in a general way about abortion and what they believed to be closely related subjects, euthanasia and genetic manipulation. At the time, Father Fiore's main concern was the conditions which led so many women to feel the need to procure abortions.

Between 1967 and 1970, Fiore found himself devoting more and more time to the abortion issue. He met Father Marx, who impressed on Fiore—as he had on the Willkes—the importance of the issue. When Fiore took charge of the Dominican Educational Association newsletter, he found himself devoting considerable space to abortion. In 1970 he was elected vice president of the board; he automatically ascended to the presidency a year later. In this position he brought in numerous speakers to talk about the dangers of abortion. At the end of his term, with the approval of the board, he founded Information of the Dominican Educational Association (IDEA), an offshoot devoted solely to the dissemination of antiabortion information.

In 1970, Fiore met Jack and Barbara Willke. He was tremendously impressed by them. No one else was doing the kind of work they were doing, in sex education and now in abortion. The Willkes and Fiore had something in common: a conviction that the key to defeating the pro-abortionists lay not so much in the logic of their arguments as in the method of presentation. In terms of educating the general public, a single bloody picture was worth more than all the volumes of sophisticated theological, philosophical, and scientific arguments they could dredge up. Fiore took note of the media techniques of the other side—the way, for example, the National Association for the Repeal of Abortion Laws always presented abortion as a neat, clean, harmless, and relatively minor procedure—and of how the national media seemed to accept this point of view. He knew that it was essential to combat this image of abortion with another. And so he put together a slide presentation of his own. It was called "The Face of Abortion," and it consisted of 24 slides, plus a voiceover. The primary objective of the presentation was to show that the fetus is not simply a blob of protoplasm.

Fiore obtained some of his fetus photographs from Dr. and Mrs. Jack C. Willke. Dr. Willke had copyrighted certain sequences of the slides, and at one point he rebuked Fiore for using them without permission. Fiore was opposed to the idea of copyrighting material that could be of general use to the movement.

The Willkes eventually marketed a slide presentation. It is called "Abortion, How It Is." There are two versions, each including the same 35 slides. The long version features a 42-minute cassette, the short one, 15 minutes. Both versions retail for $18.95, manual included. Separate versions are available in Spanish, French, Portuguese, and Italian.

While Father Fiore and the Willkes were putting together slides of dead fetuses, their mentor, Father Paul Marx, was at work on a book. To write the book, Marx attended a symposium at the International Hotel in Los Angeles on Friday, January 22, 1971—precisely two years before the Supreme Court would declare unconstitutional all laws severely restricting abortions. The program, entitled "Therapeutic Abortion: A Symposium on Implementation," attracted doctors, nurses, scholars, administrators, and politicians who favored liberalized laws and wished to provide safe, legal abortions to the most people at the least cost.

In writing for permission to attend the symposium, Father Marx had signed his name, Paul Marx, Ph.D. This was true as far as it went. He did not reveal his religious affiliation, and no one thought to ask him about it. He requested, and received, written permission to tape the proceedings. He attended, he says, "disguised as a sociologist." The result was a book about the symposium, together with Marx's critical commentary. The book is called *The Death Peddlers: War on the Unborn.* In it, Marx waxes particularly indignant when discussing the role of fellow clergy in helping young women obtain abortions. Here is his presentation of some remarks made by the Reverend J. Hugh Anwyl, director of the Los Angeles branch of the Clergy Consultation Service:

> At [Anwyl's] center, a system of contraception was always taught. After the abortion, when and if she came back for follow-up, the aborted girl was allowed to talk herself out as to her impression of hospital, doctor, and nurses. He told of one patient who, when asked what form of contraception she planned to use, replied, "Absolution." That was a new one for him, Anwyl confided amidst audience laughter. Possibly she meant abstention, he continued, but he had found, as he was sure his listeners had, that "abstention is the worst method of all." (Up to this point, the writer had always thought that a celibate abstention works rather infallibly.) Anwyl went on to say that anyone who wrote in "abstention," as obviously some did, was again contacted on the basis that "a good contraceptive system is a mark of realism and responsibility." (Not a word from this clergyman about self-control and a loving chastity!)

In *The Death Peddlers*, Marx also began to propound his theory that contraception and, more specifically, the mentality that accompanies the use of contraception lead to the easy acceptance of abortion and, therefore, more, rather than less, abortion:

> ... the foolproof contraceptive does not exist, and sociological studies have shown, almost without exception, that intensive contraceptive programs, by emphasizing the prevention of unwanted pregnancies, also reinforce an intention not to bear an unwanted child under any

circumstances; that is, there is a greater likelihood that women experiencing contraceptive failures will resort to abortion.

As a result, Marx has pursued a more vigorous campaign in recent years; not only must abortion be outlawed, but artificial birth control must be eliminated as well.

In the final sentence of his book, Marx again brings together the evils of sexual freedom and abortion: "It is sobering to envisage the dehumanizing effect on a society which has decided to condone not only the routine performance of the sexual act, whose power and mystery borrow from the power and mystery of life itself, but also the routine extermination of its young."

During the early seventies, two more books emerged that were taken to heart by the right-to-life movement, even though neither dealt directly with the question of abortion. The first, by a British chemist/economist named Dr. Colin Clark, is entitled *Population Growth: The Advantages*. The copyright on this slim paperback is held by a California attorney named Robert L. Sassone, who also wrote the introduction, proofread the manuscript, and "added reference material to the appendix." The second, *Handbook on Population*, was written by Sassone himself, and published in 1973. The aim of both volumes was to discredit those who claimed that the world was in the midst of a population explosion, and to extol the virtues of unrestricted growth. Both books deride the notion that the world is running out of resources. "No atom of metal, or anything else, is ever 'used up,'" says Clark, "except in the very rare cases of radio-activity or of nuclear reactions . . . After we have 'used' them the atoms of metal still remain in existence, in less convenient form, sometimes in unsightly dumps of old car bodies, or beer cans littering the roadside. They can, and should be, recycled for further use." He suggests putting the inhabitants of the world's prisons to work on this task.

Clark and Sassone argued that any food shortage in the world is due not to overpopulation, but to mismanagement of resources; both attempted to dismiss the notion that increases in population cancel out increased food production made possible by advanced technology. Latin America, Clark argued, is "visibly underpopulated . . . Great tracts of good land are lying uninhabited, or only sparsely cultivated." (Presumably he was talking about the rain forests, which by 1980 were disappearing at a frightening rate in response to world demand for lumber.) Sassone said, "Even India is so empty that they can keep all those useless cows and still feed their people." Sassone asserted that the entire population of the world—just under four billion people at the time—could live comfortably in the United States, enjoying, for the most part, a better standard of living than they did at the time. Both writers tended to skim lightly over the reality: that most people *were* poor and undernourished. The sacred cows of India enjoyed far better nutrition than did much of the population.

Clark and Sassone both claimed that continued population increase is necessary for continued economic growth. But Clark added another reason for governments to encourage large families. Big countries, he said, win wars over little countries:

Being a world power is not just a matter of technical advancement. Sweden and Switzerland have reached almost the same degree of technical advancement as the United States; but they are not world powers. Mexico is at a level of technical advancement not very different from that of Soviet Russia; but Soviet Russia is a world power, and Mexico is not. It is population which makes the difference. It is not so much a matter of having large numbers of recruits for the army, though that does count; nor even of having the technical ability to make modern weapons. What really makes the difference is having enough tax-payers to pay for the extraordinary costs of modern military equipment. It is true that in Russia, still more in China, tax-payers are taxed much more heavily to pay for military equipment, in relation to their incomes, than they are in the United States. But even so, if there were not so many of them, Russia and China would not be world powers.

Clark goes to great, but unconvincing, lengths, to show that Israel's victory over Arab nations with far greater populations in the Six Day War of 1967 was the exception, not the rule. "Israel was able to take advantage of the exceptionally bad leadership and disputes among themselves of her opponents. Israel's military position was shown to be much weaker in the 1973 campaign." In the first place, poor leadership usually plays a part in wartime defeat; secondly, while Israel did not win the Yom Kippur War as overwhelmingly as the Six Day War, it did not lose, either.

The right-to-life movement appropriated the population growth argument and has continued to employ it in its fight against abortion. Always there is the implication that, whatever side one is on, one had better continue to procreate, or one will be outnumbered (and overwhelmed?) by the other side. Thus, while blacks as diverse as human rights activist Dick Gregory and former National Right to Life Committee President Dr. Mildred Jefferson argue that abortion amounts to genocide of the poor and the black, Dr. and Mrs. Jack C. Willke hold that it is important for white populations to maintain and increase their numbers as well. In a booklet entitled "Marriage," the Willkes contrast population trends in America with those in less-developed nations. They note that the birth rate in the United States had dropped below replacement level by 1978, but add:

> World population is another story. Population in the underdeveloped nations of the world is increasing at a far faster rate. World population in 1930 was one billion. This doubled to two billion by 1950, to three billion by 1960, and was 3.7 billion by 1970. Some "guestimates" place world population at seven billion by A.D. 2000, while others predict a definite leveling of the curve.
>
> What are we Americans to do about people in the rest of the world? Can we remain unaffected by their overcrowding? Would it help them if we cut our growth below replacement numbers? The problem that seems to make it almost unsolvable is this: No underdeveloped people in history has ever cut its own birthrate voluntarily.
>
> Only when the standard of living of a country has risen high enough have the people voluntarily cut their birthrate.

The work of Clark and Sassone came as a response to the clamor about population growth which peaked in the sixties and early seventies with books such as Paul Ehrlich's *The Population Bomb* and reports such as the one issued by President Nixon's Commission on Population Growth and the American Future. Nixon appointed the commission in 1969. It was loaded with individuals scorned by right-to-lifers: Ehrlich, who was the founder of Zero Population Growth, Inc.; Dr. Christopher Tietze of the National Population Council; Senator Joseph Tydings of Maryland, a member of the Coalition for National Population Policy; George D. Woods, a trustee of the Rockefeller Foundation; Senator Robert Packwood, sponsor of legislation to legalize abortion nationally; and others representing Planned Parenthood, the World Population Council, and the United Nations. The chairman of the commission was none other than John D. Rockefeller III, founder and trustee of the Population Council and chairman of the Rockefeller Foundation, which had been energetically promoting family planning on the national and international levels for some time.

The commission issued its report early in 1972. Among other things, it called on the federal government to ensure that birth control counseling, devices, and oral contraceptives be made available to all Americans, especially teenagers and the poor. The commission recommended that government and private enterprise work together to provide day care centers to all families that wished to use them. In addition, there was a recommendation that the nation follow New York's lead in making available abortion on demand. (The four Catholic members of the commission dissented on this point.) The commission used two phrases which right-to-lifers immediately translated into a call for genocide. The report said population growth would have to be slowed in order to ensure that the "quality of life" would not deteriorate—and added that every child should be a "wanted child."

Leading the attack on the report, as might be expected, was the National Conference of Catholic Bishops. In a statement written by Terence Cardinal Cooke of New York, the bishops said, "We take serious exception to the general approach taken by the commission—that is, to equate quality of life simply with a lower rate of population growth on the grounds that a smaller number of people will result in greater affluence and material for all. Experience has already taught us that our social problems —poverty, disease, injustice, and violence—are not solved merely by population decrease, but require a change of heart and reordering of priorities for the entire nation." Cooke's statement was endorsed at a meeting of the Roman Catholic hierarchy in Atlanta on April 13, 1972. At the same meeting, the bishops rejected a statement that would have condemned American bombing in Southeast Asia.

President Nixon rejected the section of the report dealing with abortion. As we have seen, he subsequently sent a private letter to Cooke detailing his views and expressing his support for repeal of the New York State law.

In fact, by the end of 1972, the momentum for abortion law reform had slowed considerably, although by this time the California law was being interpreted extremely liberally, and Hawaii, Alaska, and the State of Washington had adopted laws similar to that in New York. (Washington gained its law through referendum, and remains the only state to have voted for liberalized abortion. More than 56 percent of the voters approved the new law, despite an all-out campaign waged by right-to-lifers, who put up billboards around the state which showed a bloody baby's foot and read, "Kill Referendum 20, not me." The antiabortionists also had a van which toured the state, stopping at shopping malls to invite people in to look at a display of bottled fetuses in various stages of development. This sideshow approach may have caused some viewers to wonder how much reverence for life the right-to-lifers actually had.)

Elsewhere, though, attempts to eliminate the old, restrictive laws foundered. In Ohio, Iowa, Illinois, Michigan, South Dakota, Pennsylvania, and 26 other states, legislatures voted down reform. In Ohio, the effort came in 1971; "We showed them the pictures," said Dr. Jack C. Willke, and they voted it down. The pictures were in evidence elsewhere, too. The bucket shot—fetuses in a trash can—showed up in Illinois on campaign literature calling for the defeat of legislators who favored reform. They showed up in Florida, where bishops wrote letters to their parishioners urging them to work for the defeat of reform legislation. In fact they showed up almost everywhere. By this time the National Right to Life Committee claimed chapters in "almost every state," and where there were chapters, there were pictures. State legislatures were so intimidated that in some places, they actually passed legislation tightening up the laws already on the books.

The Pennsylvania Legislature voted to outlaw abortion except when there was "reasonable medical certainty" that the mother would die otherwise; only a veto by Governor Milton Shapp prevented it from becoming law. But in Connecticut, a state that is predominantly Catholic, the governor, Thomas J. Meskill, was not similarly inclined.

In Connecticut in 1972, a federal court overturned a 122-year-old law that had allowed abortion only to save the life of the mother. Under this old law, the maximum prison term for abortionists had been two years. Angered by the court decision, the Connecticut Legislature resolved to pass an even tougher law—one that would carry a maximum *five*-year term for abortionists. During the debate on this measure, an amendment was introduced to soften it by allowing abortions in cases of rape and incest. Governor Meskill, who had studied for the priesthood, lobbied hard against these exceptions. A rape-and-incest clause, he said, would provide "a huge loophole." He added, "It amounts to abortion on demand. A woman can merely claim she was raped or in an incestuous relationship. Everyone who wants an abortion will be reporting rape." The amendment was defeated and the tough new bill became law. It, too, was challenged in court and ultimately ruled unconstitutional, but it was allowed to stay in effect pending the abortion ruling by the United States Supreme Court. Meanwhile, during the closing months of 1972, about one hundred Connecticut women per week traveled to New York for abortions.

It was the courts all over the United States that provided the right-to-lifers with their greatest frustrations, for in the courts, emotion, intimidation, bloody pictures, and threats of retribution on election day did no good. Court decisions in Vermont, Wisconsin, Florida, the District of Columbia, California, and New Jersey either voided or threw into question restrictive abortion laws. (By contrast, the Missouri Supreme Court upheld that state's life-of-the-mother-only statute.)

Late in 1971, the United States Supreme Court agreed to hear challenges to abortion laws in two states: Texas, which permitted abortion only to save the life of the mother, and Georgia, which had adopted in 1972 reform legislation similar to that endorsed by the American Law Institute and first enacted in Colorado. But the Supreme Court did not rule on the matter in 1972. The court was understaffed at the time. After the swearing-in of President Nixon's final two appointees, Lewis Powell and William Rehnquist, the court heard arguments on the cases for a second time.

CHAPTER 5

THE CATHOLIC CHURCH vs.
THE U.S. SUPREME COURT

On the morning of January 22, 1973, Father Charles Fiore awoke early to work on a paper he hoped to finish that day. He was in Berkeley, California, taking part in a seminar at the Graduate Theological Union. His mood was good. After breakfast, he returned to his room. He turned on the radio, for he enjoyed writing with music in the background. At ten or eleven o'clock—Fiore is not sure—the news came on, and he stopped to listen. What he heard horrified him.

The United States Supreme Court, by a vote of 7-2. had ruled the Texas and Georgia abortion laws unconstitutional, and in doing so had struck down all the laws in the country that fell short of allowing abortion on demand during the first trimester of pregnancy. During that time, the court said, the decision on whether or not to have an abortion rests solely with a woman and her doctor. During the second and third trimesters, the court said, states were permitted some latitude in regulating the persons and facilities involved in performing abortions. But only during the last ten weeks of pregnancy—when the fetus could be deemed capable of surviving outside the womb—would states be allowed to prohibit abortions altogether. The court angered right-to-lifers by citing a "right of privacy" not explicitly mentioned in the Constitution. Justice Harry A. Blackmun, author of the majority opinion, wrote:

> The Constitution does not explicitly mention any right of privacy. In a line of decisions, however, the Court has recognized that a right of personal privacy, or a guarantee of certain areas or zones of privacy, does exist under the Constitution.
>
> This right of privacy, whether it be founded in the 14th Amendment's concept of personal liberty and restrictions upon state action, as we feel it is, or . . . in the Ninth Amendment's reservation of rights to the people, is broad enough to encompass a woman's decision whether or not to terminate her pregnancy.

The only state statutes the decision left standing were those in New York, Alaska, Hawaii, and Washington—all of which already permitted abortion on demand.

As he heard the news, Father Fiore grew angry, but this feeling faded, to be replaced by a sensation of illness. He had been involved in the abortion struggle for more than five years now, and he knew what lay ahead. That the battle would be long he took for granted, but he knew it would be a bitter, bitter fight. (It never occurred to him that there would *not* be a fight.) But mostly, he mourned for the millions of unborn babies who would be killed in the interim.

As the morning went on he experienced a cycle of moods: anger again, then revulsion, disgust, and despondency. But also there came a growing determination that, by God, he and his cohorts were going to turn this thing around. A day or two later, when he met with the local press, he announced that the Supreme Court, by taking the decision out of the hands of the individual states where it rightfully belonged, and by exercising "'raw judicial power'" (as Justice Byron R. White characterized the decision in his dissent), had flung down the gauntlet. The only recourse left to those who disagreed with the decision, he said, was to push for an amendment to the United States Constitution that would define human life as beginning at the moment of fertilization.

A few days later, Fiore picked up a copy of the *New York Times* and gritted his teeth as he read an editorial which advised that now that the court had spoken, it would be in the best interests of the country for all citizens to abide by that decision.[1] The *Times*, he knew, had done everything in its power to promote a proabortion mentality. He, Fiore, would now do everything in *his* power to see that the victory was temporary.

While Fiore listened to the news in his room at Berkeley, Dr. Jack C. Willke sat in the anteroom of a radio station in Houston, Texas, waiting to go on the air. The Willkes were involved in the abortion issue almost full-time now. They were master educators, traveling around the country, teaching others how to get across the right-to-life message and how to set up local right-to-life chapters. Usually Barbara came along on these trips; this was one of the few times Jack was on the road alone. With him in the anteroom was a representative of a local Planned Parenthood organization; the two were scheduled to go on the air together, and answer questions. As they waited, an employee of the station came in with a tear sheet from United Press International. The employee said, "I thought you two would be interested in this—it's on your issue."

Willke remembers that moment:

> We knew that the decision was in the court . . . we knew that these cases had been appealed and that there was a mixed bag of reaction to them, some in our favor, some against us—but nobody dreamt—not even the most avid proabortion person—that we would come down with loss of legal personhood and abortion on demand till birth. Nobody dreamt that that would happen.

In any case, for the next few days Willke was an extremely busy man. Between the time he received the news and the time he left Houston late the next day for Dallas, he appeared on fourteen radio and television shows. It got so hectic that while he was on a radio call-in show, a television crew came in and filmed him answering the questions. The Supreme Court decision kicked the Willkes' already flourishing careers as antiabortionists into high gear; they were on the road a total of three months out of the next twelve.

But for the next three years, it was the bishops of the Catholic Church in America who carried on the strongest and loudest resistance to the Supreme Court ruling. On the day the decision was handed down, Cardinal Cooke of New York said, "In spite of this horrifying decision, the American people must rededicate themselves to the protection of the sacredness of all human life. I hope and pray that our citizens will do all in their power to reverse this injustice to the rights of the unborn child."[2] John Cardinal

Krol, Archbishop of Philadelphia and president of the National Conference of Catholic Bishops, asserted, "No court and no legislature in the land can make something evil become something good. Abortion at any stage of pregnancy is evil. This is not a question of sectarian morality but instead concerns the law of God and the basis of civilized society."[3] (This last sentence is puzzling, since the very bases for sectarian divisions have been different interpretations of the law of God.) Two days later, the National Conference of Catholic Bishops officially declared war on the decision, and their call to battle was not limited to Catholics: "Although as a result of the Court decision abortion may be legally permissible, it is still morally wrong, and no court opinion can change the law of God prohibiting the taking of human life. Therefore, as religious leaders, we cannot accept the Court's judgment and we urge people not to follow its reasoning or conclusions." (As always, there were factions on the right which felt the bishops had not gone far enough; one Catholic laymen's group, the Society for the Christian Commonwealth, called for the excommunication of Justice William J. Brennan, a Catholic who had, nevertheless, sided with the majority.)

Throughout 1973 the bishops continued their fusillade. On February 14, they announced that any Catholic involved in any phase of abortion would be subject to immediate excommunication: "Those who obtain an abortion, and those who persuade others to have an abortion, and those who perform the abortion procedure are guilty of breaking God's law."[5] On October 7, from the pulpit of Saint Patrick's Cathedral in New York City, Cardinal Cooke formally launched a new "Respect Life" program, which would involve all 160 dioceses and 18,000 parishes across the United States. And on November 13, the National Conference of Catholic Bishops issued a resolution calling on Catholics to embark on a political crusade at the grass-roots level to achieve a constitutional amendment outlawing abortion:

> ... we remind our people that the passage of the amendment will require concerted and continued efforts on their part to convince the Congress and American people of its absolute necessity. Specifically, we urge public information programs and petitions to state legislatures to memorialize Congress in behalf of a pro-life amendment. In all of this, well-planned and coordinated political organization by citizens at the national, state, and local levels are of the highest importance. Our system of government requires citizen participation, and in this case there is a *moral imperative* for political activity.[6]

This was the first time the bishops officially called for *political* action; it would be another two years before they produced a detailed plan for such action. There was, inconveniently, a federal regulation prohibiting religious organizations from endorsing political candidates, and the penalty for violation of this regulation—loss of tax-exempt status—would have been severe, particularly as applied to the Catholic Church. Nevertheless, on the local level, some church officials were bolder than their superiors in Washington.

New Jersey is one of the few states to hold elections for state offices during odd-numbered years. In 1973 the candidates for governor were Brendan Byrne, a liberal

Democrat, and Charles Sandman, an archconservative Republican who, a year later, would become one of President Richard M. Nixon's staunchest defenders during the House Judiciary Committee impeachment hearings. In the 1973 Republican gubernatorial primary, Sandman defeated the incumbent, moderate Republican William J. Cahill. In this effort he was backed by a national coalition of right-wing groups, including the Young Americans for Freedom, the American Conservative Union, and Americans for Constitutional Action. The John Birch Society and the reactionary radio preacher the Reverend Carl McIntyre also endorsed Sandman. To this list of sponsors, substantial elements of the Catholic Church in New Jersey tacitly (though never directly) added their names.

Throughout the campaign, Sandman made abortion a major issue. At a right-to-life rally in Branch Brook Park, Newark, Sandman promised to force House Judiciary Committee Chairman Peter Rodino, a fellow New Jerseyan, to hold hearings on a human life amendment. If he were elected governor, he said, "no public money will be appropriated for mass murder—for that is what abortion is."

On the Sunday before the general election, brochures were distributed at Catholic churches in Bergen County and the Democratic areas of Hudson, Essex, Passaic, Morris, and Mercer counties. The brochures said the Democratic candidate for governor, Brendan Byrne, "feels that it is an individual's right to kill the unborn." (Byrne, in fact, had said that he was personally opposed to abortions, and that he would support the holding of hearings on a human life amendment. But he had stopped far short of calling abortion murder.) At some of the churches, a separate list of candidates for the state legislature was also distributed. Each candidate was designated either "pro-life" or "pro-abortion."

Thus, elements of the church had made a choice that was to become more and more frequent in subsequent years: to back a candidate who opposed virtually everything the church stood for in the areas of social programs and individual rights, simply because that candidate opposed abortion. But in this case the church was divided. The distribution of the brochure had not been authorized by the state's bishop, and Monsignor Harold Murray, secretary of the National Catholic Conference Social Development and World Peace Department, called the brochure "unfair" and "distorted." He added that the distribution at various churches "put the church in a very difficult position, that of seeming to support the contents of the brochure." In any case, Sandman was a weak candidate and the brochures did him no good; Byrne defeated him by a two-to-one margin.

While the church was divided over its political activities in New Jersey, such was not the case in Missouri, where a united church exerted a strong influence on the political process. In fact, in the days immediately following January 22, 1973, the church distributed news of the abortion decisions because two other major news stories dominated the newspapers that week. Only a few hours after the ruling was released, former President Lyndon B. Johnson died of a heart attack at his Texas ranch. On the following day, in Paris, representatives of the United States, South Vietnam, and North Vietnam signed a treaty that would bring to an end United States military involvement in Vietnam.

On Saturday night, January 27, Loretto Wagner of St. Louis went to church. There would be a special mass, and she was in the choir. She brought with her feelings of relief and of thanksgiving. At last, the Vietnam war seemed to be over.

But the priest on the pulpit that night did not share her mood. This was not the parish priest, but a guest. Loretto Wagner does not remember his name; she remembers that he was an old man, and an angry one. In a thundering voice he proclaimed, "All you people who are rejoicing over the war should be in mourning over what the Supreme Court did." He asked, "Where are all these people who were out protesting in the streets against the war? They should be out there demonstrating against this atrocious crime, the atrocity of this decision!"

Loretto Wagner, the mother of six children, was then two weeks shy of her thirty-eighth birthday. She had grown up in St. Louis, and gone to parochial schools: at Xavier High School an elderly nun had alerted her to the problems that Negroes were having in the supposedly democratic United States of America. Young Loretto knew something should be done to correct this situation, but when she graduated from high school it was only 1951; by the time the civil rights movement was in full swing, a few years later, she was married and pregnant. She always regretted her inability to get involved.

Prior to that Saturday in January 1973, she had not thought much about abortion, although she knew she was against it. She had *always* been against it; in school it was taken for granted that abortion was wrong; nobody ever talked about it. Since there were no specific injunctions against abortion during her education, Wagner reasons that it could not have been her Catholic background that set her against it. Abortion was just—well, *wrong*. In 1972 she had seen a brochure written by a Baptist preacher from Texas that gave a graphic description of abortion—cutting up the baby, crushing its head, rhetoric of that sort. And she had gone as far as sending away to California for a bumper sticker that said "Abortion Is Murder." She pasted the bumper sticker on her car, and thought she had done her part for the issue.

But now, as the voice of the old priest thundered around her, she knew that she had not done enough. As she left the church she told a friend, "I don't know what I'm going to do, but I'm going to do something," for she had been given a second chance to help her fellow man. She had missed out on the Negro, but would not allow the opportunity to save unborn babies pass her by. As time went on, she devoted more and more time to the cause; by 1980 she was on the board of directors of Missouri Citizens for Life, and had been arrested several times for sitting in at abortion clinics.

Just as the church alerted Loretto Wagner to the evils of abortion, it alerted thousands of others. In March 1973, John Cardinal Carberry convened a meeting of the diocesan representatives of the Saint Louis Archdiocese; more than 1,100 people showed up. The cardinal stressed the need for a human life amendment. He pledged $20,000 from the archdiocese to help accomplish this goal. In addition, he announced the establishment of an elaborate political and educational apparatus for pro-life activities. At the apex was the cardinal; beneath him, a five-man archdiocesan committee for pro-life activities, and beneath that, pro-life committees in every parish. Each parish had two cochairmen, who were given a handbook with information and suggestions for raising funds and educating citizens about the evils of abortion. Meetings of the parish chairmen were held every two months, and a telephone tree was set up to ensure instant communication with the chairmen. A speakers' bureau was established to supply parish groups with a stream of pro-life lecturers, and a "literature committee" was set up to keep the speakers up to date on the latest developments. In addition, a bulletin dealing with right-to-life matters was placed inside regular parish bulletins once a month. There were also bumper stickers and pro-life bracelets.

Beyond that, there was political action. According to a pro-life brochure issued by the archdiocese in 1976, "Early in the history of the committee, it was realized that we would have to enlist the cooperation of politicians at every level to accomplish the legislative goals established by the Cardinal's address. Maps and charts were developed showing the relationship of parishes to Congressional districts and Missouri legislative districts." Citizens were encouraged to keep in constant touch with their elected officials.

The results of this campaign were dramatic. In its 1974 session, the Missouri Legislature passed a tough antiabortion bill. Among other things, the measure specified that women needed the consent of their husbands in order to have an abortion and that single women under the age of eighteen needed the consent of their parents, and it outlawed saline abortions after the twelfth week of pregnancy. (The United States Supreme Court ruled these provisions unconstitutional in 1976.) The Missouri Legislature also became the first in the nation to issue a call for a Constitutional Convention to draft a human life amendment.

While the bishops in Washington, D.C., were two years behind Cardinal Carberry in terms of organizing the troops, they did engage in direct political action against abortion. On March 4, 1974, four cardinals appeared before the United States Senate's Subcommittee on Constitutional Amendments to advocate a human life amendment. This was an unprecedented event. In later years, the Catholic hierarchy would attempt to justify its political activism on behalf of the antiabortion cause by citing its support of social programs and civil rights legislation in the past. But never had four cardinals—or any officials of the hierarchy, for that matter—deemed it appropriate to testify before a congressional committee in support of a voting rights act, or legislation mandating equal access to housing or public facilities.

At the time there were several versions of the proposed human life amendment before the committee. One would have permitted abortions to terminate pregnancies resulting from rape or incest. Another would have set the beginning of human life at implantation, rather than fertilization, thus ensuring that certain birth control devices such as the intrauterine device and some low-estrogen pills (which may work by preventing implantation, and thus are technically abortifacients) would remain legal. The most severe version would have permitted abortion only if the life of the mother were in danger. None of these was acceptable to the cardinals.

The four who testified were John Cardinal Cody of Chicago, John Cardinal Krol of Philadelphia, Timothy Cardinal Manning of Los Angeles, and Humberto Cardinal Medeiros of Boston. Cardinal Krol issued the by now ritual denial that the church was attempting to impose its views on other Americans: "We speak as American citizens who are free to express our view." But he acknowledged later that they spoke not simply as American citizens, but as conveyors of the official view of a church with 49 million members.

It fell to Cardinal Medeiros to explain why—to be acceptable to the church—a human life amendment must not permit abortion in *any* circumstances, not even to save the life of the mother:

> As for an amendment which would generally prohibit abortion but permit it in certain exceptional circumstances, such as when a woman's life is considered to be threatened, the Catholic Conference does not endorse such an approach in principle and could not conscientiously support it.
>
> The teaching of the Catholic Church regarding abortion is very clear: "For God, the Lord of life, has conferred on men the surpassing ministry of safeguarding life—a ministry which must be fulfilled in a manner which is worthy of man. Therefore from the moment of its conception life must be guarded with the greatest care, while abortion and infanticide are unspeakable crimes."[4]

This position would be reconfirmed in Rome a few months

later; in November, Pope Paul VI approved a document specifying that neither the threat to a mother's life nor any other extenuating circumstances justify abortion.

As in the case of birth control, the church was justifying its stand, not on the basis of Scripture, but on the basis of church doctrine. Therefore, while it was, indeed, true that abortion was not solely a Catholic issue, the Catholic Church was arguing its case on specifically Catholic grounds.[5]

It was not surprising that Cardinal Medeiros delivered the church's hard line on abortion to the subcommittee. This was not the first time he had spoken out strongly on the subject, nor would it be the last. Nor had Medeiros ever been shy about plunging into the political arena.

His father was a farmer in the village of Arrifes, in the Portuguese Azores. Humberto was born October 6, 1915, and he came to the United States at the age of fifteen. He did not enter high school until three years later; eventually he went on to Catholic University in Washington, and the Gregorian University in Rome. In 1960 he became a parish priest and chancery official in Fall River, Massachusetts, a predominantly blue-collar city with a large Portuguese population. Six years later he was made bishop of the diocese of Brownsville, Texas. Then, late in the summer of 1970, the beloved Richard Cardinal Cushing of Boston became too ill to continue his duties, and Medeiros was chosen to lead the second largest (to Chicago) archdiocese in the country, with its 410 parishes and nearly two million Catholics.

On September 13, after his appointment had been announced but three weeks before taking over as archbishop, Medeiros gave a television interview in which he said he fully backed the views of the pope on abortion. He also said the church should be involved in politics "whenever there is a moral issue." Once installed, Medeiros lost little time emphasizing the evils of abortion. On December 28, 1970, in Hanover, Massachusetts, he celebrated a mass with five other priests to protest the increased acceptance of abortion by society. He said attempts to liberalize abortion laws amounted to "a step backward" and "a new barbarism." The vigor of his attack led to a protest by leaders of other religious denominations. The Reverend Robert N. West, international leader of the Unitarian Universalist Association, condemned him for "hurling epithets such as 'barbarian' and 'enemies of life,'" and said, "It is unfortunate that opponents of reform have been reduced to frantic and fanatic name-calling."[6] And Rabbi Roland B. Gittelsohn of Boston's Temple Israel said the archbishop spoke "as if all moral rights were on one side of the question."[7] But Medeiros was undeterred. When Cardinal Cooke of New York called on him to deliver an address at Saint Patrick's Cathedral on the Fourth of July, 1971, Medeiros announced sternly that 165,000 human lives had been "snuffed out by legalized abortion in New York City last year."

Given Medeiros's hard-line attitude and his disposition to speak out frequently on abortion, it was natural that the bishops would turn to him when they needed a witness at a congressional hearing. Yet Medeiros was not always so eloquent in defending innocent lives. Only a few months after the hearings, Medeiros demonstrated convincingly that a baby with the wrong connections would never make it to Heaven—not through the Boston Archdiocese, in any case.

In the summer of 1974, not long after Medeiros delivered his stirring testimony on behalf of the unborn, a
child was born to Mrs. Carol Morreale, of Marlboro,
.Massachusetts. Mrs. Morreale normally attended the
Immaculate Conception church in that town; she made an
appointment to have her son, Nathaniel Ryan Morreale,
baptized there on Sunday, August 11, at 2:00 P.M. But
only 40 minutes before the designated time, she received a
call from the parish priest, the Reverend John Roussin.
Father Roussin informed her that there would be a problem. In fact, he said, he would not perform the baptism,
because the mother was guilty of a profound transgression
in the eyes of the church. She was an acknowledged supporter of a gentleman named Bill Baird.

Bill Baird is a crusader. He is not a subtle person. He
believes that birth control should be available to anyone
who wants it, and that any woman who wants an abortion
should be able to obtain one. Since 1965 he has been
traveling around the country saying these things. He has
never been shy about labeling the Catholic Church the
prime enemy of the reproductive rights of women. On December 30, 1973, he called Cardinal Medeiros "public
enemy number one of the rights of women."[8] And in late
May 1974, he was in Marlboro to take on the Reverend
John J. Roussin, who was openly backing a proposed ordi-
nance to outlaw abortion clinics in that town.

In early June a black flag appeared on the flagpole outside the Immaculate Conception church. A sign said, "This
flag flies in silent protest against the presence in Marlboro
of Mr. William Baird, a proabortionist activist and a ped-
dler of death."

Baird responded by sending a telegram to Cardinal Medeiros. In it, he threatened to sue the church for libel and slander unless Roussin apologized for the sign and the flag. Baird announced that he would use the money he expected to win from the suit to set up a "free Bill Baird catholic (with a small 'c,' meaning universal) Abortion Center."

Roussin was not pleased. And so, when it came time to baptize someone twice removed from his antagonist—the son of Mrs. Morreale—Roussin refused. Cardinal Medeiros concurred in this decision. (The church has a standing rule that a priest need not baptize a child if he believes the parents are incapable of providing a good Catholic upbringing; thus, the church writes off and condemns what it considers poor risks. The innocence of the child does not seem to cause the bishops much concern.) An emissary from the archdiocese, the Reverend Francis X. Meeham, visited Mrs. Morreale and, in front of fifteen witnesses, told her that Nathan could not be baptized in Marlboro, the Archdiocese of Boston, or the Commonwealth of Massachusetts. Bill Baird subsequently sent another telegram to Medeiros, asking him to baptize the baby personally; in reply there was only silence. Eventually a dissident priest from New York City baptized Nathan Morreale.

The dissident priest, the Reverend Joseph O'Rourke, was thirty-six years old and experienced at bucking his superiors. A member of the West Side Community of the Society of Jesus, he was a veteran of the civil rights and antiwar movements, and on one occasion was arrested with Father Daniel Berrigan for breaking into a government building. He believed, among other things, that priests should not be celibate—"I don't think you can really be a priest and celibate"—and that women should be allowed to become priests. He performed the baptism on August 20, 1974.

Justice—or, at least, retribution—is swift in the Catholic Church. Barely two weeks later Father O'Rourke was stripped of his Society of Jesus (S.J.) title; he remained a priest, but was suddenly without a bishop or an assignment. There had been no hearing, no due process. He subsequently filed a 30-page appeal to the Vatican and was turned down; he then wrote directly to Pope Paul VI, who received his message in silence. O'Rourke heard indirectly that the case was closed.

Thus, Cardinal Medeiros (along with his fellow bishops and the pope) had put an interesting twist on the teachings of the church. Recall that at the hearing on a human life amendment Medeiros had quoted church doctrine: "'Therefore from the moment of its conception life must be guarded with the greatest care . . .'" He had already demonstrated that the life of the mother was worth less, in his eyes and the eyes of the church, than the life of the fetus. And now, in Marlboro, he showed that the spiritual, if not physical, life of Nathan Morreale was of less concern to him than a vendetta. Only the intervention of Father Roussin gave Nathan the freedom to become a Catholic in the fullest sense—to participate in the rituals of the church and to marry in a Catholic ceremony.

In addition to local efforts to punish abortion supporters like Mrs. Morreale, the Catholic hierarchy continued escalating its attack on the Supreme Court decision, although the bishops were now receiving some severe criticism, not only from leaders of other religions (which was to be expected) but from leaders of right-to-life groups who were eager to project themselves as multidenominational. At the March 4 hearing in Washington, Catholicism was not the only religion represented. But the cardinals made their appearance early in the day; other religious leaders testified late in the afternoon, after the television cameras had been packed up. The result, said Jean Garton, lay woman from the Missouri Synod of the Lutheran Church, was a "tactical disaster." Following the Washington hearing, the bishops also announced their intention of establishing within the United States Catholic Conference a National Committee for a Human Life Amendment— something deplored by the chairman of the National Right to Life Committee, Marjorie Mecklenberg, a United Methodist. Judy Fink, National Right to Life Committee secretary and a member of Baptists for Life, said the Catholic Church's "separatist attitude can only serve the purpose of the abortion groups who want to prove once and for all that abortion is truly a Catholic issue."

The Catholic Church's pronouncements about abortion provoked other religious bodies to openly criticize their tactics. Only a week before the hearings, the 200-member general board of the American Baptist Churches passed a resolution accusing the bishops of attempting to "coerce the conscience and personal freedom" of Americans through what the Baptists called a "crusade" against abortion. The resolution added that the human life amendment which the Catholic hierarchy supported would "violate theological and moral sensitivities, and hence the freedom, of other church bodies." In May, representatives of the

U.S. Catholic Conference and the American Baptist Church met, but did not settle the matter. Each side issued a statement saying the meeting had been helpful, and the issue was papered over. But the strain remained; a subsequent meeting in December 1975 also failed to resolve the conflict.

By that time, the National Conference of Catholic Bishops had issued a national battle plan for fighting abortion—a plan which potentially enlisted every parishioner in every church in every diocese in the country in the revolution against the Supreme Court. It was called the Pastoral Plan for Pro-Life Activities, and it provided specific roles for the bishops in Washington, Catholic officials at the regional and diocesan levels, parish priests, and Catholic laymen. It was approved unanimously at the annual meeting of the NCCB in Washington, D.C., in November 1975.[9]

The plan included, first, an educational and public relations effort, which was to be carried out by "all who participate in the church's educational ministry," notably:

—Priests and religious exercising their teaching responsibility in the pulpit, in other teaching assignments, and through parish programs.

—All Church-sponsored or identifiably Catholic organizations, national, regional, diocesan, and parochial, carrying on continuing education efforts that emphasize the moral prohibition of abortion and the reasons for carrying this teaching into the public policy area.

—Schools, CCD [Confraternity of Christian Doctrine— is geared toward teenagers, and includes catechism classes] and other church-sponsored educational agencies providing moral teaching bolstered by medical, legal, and sociological data, in the schools, etc. . . .

—Church-related social service and health agencies carrying continuing education efforts through seminars and other appropriate programs, and by publicizing programs and services offering alternatives to abortion.

The second part of the plan, entitled "Pastoral Care," emphasized forgiveness, and was to be carried out mainly by the clergy. "Granting that the grave sin of abortion is symptomatic of many human problems, which often remain unsolved for the individual women, it is important that we realize that God's mercy is always available and without limit, that Christian life can be restored and renewed through the sacraments, and that union with God can be accomplished despite the problems of human existence." (There is no direct reference in the Pastoral Plan to the numerous warnings by various bishops of excommunication for any Catholic involved with abortion.) In order to dissuade pregnant women from considering abortion, the plan calls for "adequate education and material sustenance . . . for women so they may choose motherhood responsibly and freely in accord with the basic commitment to the sanctity of life." The plan then calls for material, nutritional, and spiritual care for these women, and "extension of adoption and foster care facilities to those who need them," as well as "continued efforts to remove the social stigma that is visited on the woman who is pregnant out of wedlock and on her child." In addition, there is a call for "special understanding, encouragement, and support for victims of rape." (The plan offers no details about how one first forces a woman to carry to term a fetus she conceived against her will, and with a man she despises—and then, having violated her free will as certainly as the rapist himself, one offers understanding, encouragement, and support, without being equally despised.)

The third section of the plan was purely political in nature, and ranged far beyond the confines of the Catholic Church. Its ultimate goal was the passage of a human life amendment; in the meantime, it called for "passage of federal and state laws and adoption of administrative policies that will restrict the practice of abortion as much as possible; continual research into and refinement and precise interpretation of *Roe* and *Doe* [the cases decided by the Supreme Court were known as *Roe* v. *Wade* and *Doe* v. *Bolton*] and subsequent court decisions, and support for legislation that provides alternatives to abortion." To accomplish these goals, the plan called for the Catholic hierarchy in each state to, among other things, "evaluate progress in the dioceses and congressional districts." Pro-life committees at the diocese level would "encourage the development of 'grass roots' political action organizations," "maintain communication with the National Committee for a Human Life Amendment in regard to federal activity, so as to provide instantaneous information concerning local senators and representatives," and "develop close relationships with each senator or representative." Pro-life committees at the parish level were to serve as information conduits for the committees at the diocese level; in addition, they were to "prudently convince others—Catholics and non-Catholics—of the reasons for the necessity of a constitutional amendment to provide a base for legal protection for the unborn."

An early draft of the Pastoral Plan, not approved by a majority of the bishops, called for a great deal of direct lobbying. In addition, the bishops attempted to put some (but not much) distance between themselves and the people who would be doing most of the grass-roots political work. From a political standpoint, probably the most significant declaration in the final version of the plan was the following:

> . . . it is absolutely necessary to encourage the development in each congressional district of an identifiable, tightly knit, and well organized pro-life unit. This unit can be described as a public interest group or a citizens lobby. No matter what it is called:
>
> (a) its task is essentially political, that is, to organize people to help persuade the elected representatives; and
>
> (b) its range of action is limited, that is, it is focussed on passing a constitutional amendment.
>
> As such, the congressional district pro-life group differs from the diocesan, regional or parish pro-life coordinator or committee, whose task is pedagogic and motivational, not simply political, and whose range of action includes a variety of efforts calculated to reverse the present atmosphere of permissiveness with respect to abortion. Moreover, it is an agency of the citizens—operated, controlled, and financed by these same citizens. It is not an agency of the Church, nor is it operated, controlled, or financed by the Church.

Thus, officially, the church was restricting itself to

"encouragement" of politically active right-to-life groups, but clearly, many of the citizens recruited for these groups would be in constant contact with the church—at least on Sundays.

During the late 1970s, the church, and particularly individual clergymen, became increasingly involved in the support of conservative candidates who endorsed a human life amendment. This troubled liberal Catholics. In the November 10, 1978, edition of the *National Catholic Reporter*, writer Mark Winiarski posed the dilemma:

> The Catholic voter increasingly faces decisions between two candidates: one, anti-abortion but allied with a politics that would restrict government aid to the less fortunate; another, who articulates social justice teachings but would allow abortion to continue. And what is the church's answer to him or her?

In the vast majority of cases, the answer was: oppose abortion at all costs. Thus, in April 1980, the Reverend Thomas H. Burns of St. John deBritto Church in Brittan, South Dakota, wrote a letter to other priests in that state in which he endorsed Larry Shoemaker, a conservative Democrat opposing Senator George McGovern in the state primary:

> South Dakotans are angry. . and scared.
>
> Inflation is at its highest point since World War II. Interest rates have soared to 20%. America is suffering from a moral decline.
>
> *And what has George McGovern done?*

He has voted for inflationary deficit spending every year he has been in office.

He has consistently voted to weaken our national defense.

He has repeatedly voted for the federal funding of abortions.

While Reverend Burns attacked McGovern with a shotgun blast of conservative gripes, a certain high-ranking prelate in the East took more specific aim. The week before the Massachusetts state primary, Humberto Cardinal Medeiros wrote an open letter to Catholics asking them to vote against candidates who supported legalized abortion:

> The Second Vatican Council declares that abortion is "an unspeakable crime." Those who make abortions possible by law—such as legislators and those who promote, defend, and elect these same lawmakers—cannot separate themselves totally from the guilt which accompanies this horrendous crime and deadly sin. If you are for true human freedom—and for life—you will follow your conscience when you vote, you will vote to save "our children, *born and unborn.*"

The letter was aimed at candidates in two congressional races: Freshman Representative James Shannon, a pro-choice Democrat and a Catholic, in the Fifth District, and State Representative Barney Frank in the Fourth District. The Fourth District race was of particular symbolic importance, since the winner would replace Representative Robert F. Drinan, the Jesuit priest who had occupied the seat since 1971. Drinan, an outspoken liberal, had been a consistent supporter of federal funding for abortion. In the spring of 1980, Pope John Paul II had ordered him not to seek re-election, and Drinan had reluctantly acceded to the pope's wishes. Much to the dismay of Cardinal Medeiros, Drinan was energetically campaigning for Barney Frank, a Jewish liberal and an ardent supporter of abortion rights.

The cardinal's attempt to influence the elections failed; both Shannon and Frank won their primary battles and went on to victory in the general elections. But the letter helped to cement the formidable, if informal, alliance of the Catholic Church, the increasingly active fundamentalist Protestant "pro-family" movement, and the New Right. Upon hearing of the letter, Conservative Caucus head Howard Phillips remarked, "I see Cardinal Medeiros has joined the Moral Majority. This is an extremely exciting development."

CHAPTER 6

TWO WOMEN FROM TEXAS

The right-to-life movement *outside* the Catholic Church became visible nationally in 1974 and 1975 due to the efforts of two women from the State of Texas. One, Mildred Faye Jefferson, is a doctor, the other, Nellie Gray, a lawyer. Jefferson is black, Gray is white. Jefferson was married (and divorced), while Gray remains single. Jefferson severed her ties with organized religion, while Gray embraces the Catholic Church with a passion. Jefferson sees herself as an accommodator, reaching out to the broadest possible spectrum of people sympathetic to the antiabortion cause; Nellie Gray takes the hard line of the Catholic Church: no human life amendment is acceptable unless it outlaws abortion under all circumstances, even including a threat to the life of the mother. Both women entertain apocalyptic visions of what might happen to supporters of abortion in the wake of the passage of a human life amendment.

On June 27, 1980, Dr. Mildred Faye Jefferson spoke disparagingly of the class of people known to her audience as secular humanists. Her audience, in this case, consisted of about two hundred supporters of the Life Amendment Political Action Committee (LAPAC), an organization more hard-line on the abortion issue than the National Right to Life Committee. Dr. Jefferson, a former president of the National Right to Life Committee, was a member of the board of directors of LAPAC.

She is a dazzling speaker. Her voice, relatively low in pitch, is clear and strong, and her enunciation is precise. Her father and grandfather were preachers, and there is in Mildred Jefferson's delivery an arresting quality that one associates with black Baptist preachers, but unlike them, Jefferson always has the appearance of being firmly in control. Perhaps it is this aura of control that more than anything else contributes to the hypnotic quality of her delivery. In any case, on the evening of June 27 she told her audience that the basic conflict in which they were engaged pitted the philosophy that Man is created in the image of God—"the Judeo-Christian consensus"—against the philosophy based on the premise that Man came about as an accident of nature, and therefore is accountable only to himself. This latter philosophy, she said,

> ... puts so much focus on Man and ... selfhood that in order to show this new authority, the only way it can be expressed is in terms of the destructive impulse—the ethics of selfhood—freedom of abortion; freedom of suicide; freedom of euthanasia. What demands! The kind of freedom that can only lead to the destruction of those who are claiming that freedom.
>
> Now, why don't we, as I have so often recommended in the past, simply let them act out their destructive impulses, so that if indeed they do believe what they are saying, they would be removed from our society?

Dr. Jefferson paused dramatically, then answered her own question, pausing again between each of the last three words: "Because it *takes*... *too*... *long!*" The audience laughed appreciatively, and she continued: "By the time they finish carrying it through they've done too much damage. And the worst damage they could have done is to seize that emotional control that turned the family of this nation against its own young."

Four days later, in Washington, D.C., Nellie Gray raised the specter of a Nuremberg-like trial at which senators and representatives who vote for government funding for abortion, or who oppose a human life amendment, would be brought to account for their "crimes." Testifying before the House Appropriations Defense Subcommittee, Gray, president of an organization called The March for Life, Inc., said,

> The core issue before America is whether it is right or wrong for anyone—in private or public—to kill an innocent preborn child? The answer is obvious: it is wrong—it is a crime against humanity—for anyone to kill an innocent preborn child, and it is wrong for anyone to direct such killing, and it is wrong for anyone to pay for such killing.

She cited the charter of the Tribunal at Nuremberg, which specified that the perpetrator of a crime against humanity is not considered free of responsibility for that act simply because the act was in accordance with official government policy at the time, and she concluded:

> Therefore, it follows clearly that merely because abortion —a crime against humanity—can be said to be "legal"

in our country today, does not make the act of abortion less inhumane or less a crime against humanity. Further, anyone in public or private life, in elected or appointed positions, who participates in or even supports abortion is open to the serious question of accountability for the crimes against humanity now going on in our country through abortion. Those organizations who advocate, participate in, propagandize, and lobby for abortion, along with their membership, are equally open to being declared criminal.

In effect, Nellie Gray was telling the committee members that she would do her best to bring to trial any of *them* who supported abortion, once a human life amendment had been added to the Constitution.

Nellie Gray was born in Big Spring, in West Texas, in 1924. After attending public schools there she went one year to Texas State College for Women, in Denton, before leaving school in 1942 to become secretary to the commanding officer of the Army Air Force bombardier school back in Big Spring. Two years later she joined the Army, where she continued as a secretary while serving hitches in Savannah, Georgia, and San Antonio, Texas, and an overseas stint in Paris. During this time she achieved the rank of corporal. In 1946, when the war was over, she returned to Texas State on the G.I. Bill and went on to earn a B.S. in business administration and an M.A. in economics. In 1950 she went to work for the government again, first as an economic research assistant for the State Department—a job that took her to postwar Germany for two years—and then, for seventeen years, as a manpower legislation expert with the Department of Labor. Meanwhile, she earned a law degree at Georgetown University Law Center night school. She has viewed herself as a liberated woman since the day she was born, and scoffs at modern-day feminists: "If equal work and equal pay and these sort of things are what they're looking for, or equal opportunity, the Army was available long before the women's lib movement came along. Law School was available long before women's lib came along...and so I don't consider this as a women's lib movement. There is nothing liberating about it. It is absolute slavery to a Sodom and Gomorrah mentality, and it does absolutely nothing but denigrate women." She pauses. "Them and their free and open sex without marriage and so forth. I think the whole notion, the International Women's Year promoting gay rights and lesbians and so forth down in Houston at federal expense shows to me that these are just totally misguided people."

In the late sixties, Nellie Gray became aware that attempts were under way to liberalize the nation's abortion laws. This angered her. It was a straight gut reaction: *you just don't kill babies.* In 1970, when the United States Supreme Court upheld a restrictive abortion law in Washington, D.C., which permitted abortion only in cases where the life or health of the mother was endangered, she saw the decision in a negative light. The court, after all, had said that some abortions are all right. Still, when the Supreme Court announced that it would consider the challenges to abortion laws in Georgia and Texas, she felt comfortable, because she was sure the court could do nothing but recognize the right to life of the fetus, or, as she thought of it, "the pre-born child." She likens January 22, 1973, to Pearl Harbor Day; it shook her sense of security in the same way. She thought of how the government of the United States once had treated slaves as less than human, and how, prior to the Holocaust, the Nazis had designated Jews, Gypsies, and other non-Aryan races as not fully human. Now the same thing was happening to the fetus, the embryo, the zygote. Theologians and philosophers throughout recorded history had been unable to determine when human life begins, but Nellie Gray knew. It was more than an opinion—she *knew*. And common sense told her that if the government one day were able to declare fetuses nonpersons, then another day the same thing might happen to the elderly, or the retarded; the possibilities were endless and appalling. It was beyond her comprehension that a country which had fought a war to save the Jews (sic) and which had spent years expanding the rights of blacks and other minorities, could at the same time allow the killing of babies. In June 1973 she made a decision. She would quit her government job, begin a private law practice (which she never got around to starting), and dedicate the rest of her time to the cause of saving unborn babies.

She started her right-to-life activities with a few appearances on radio and television shows, and became known to others in the movement. Within months, this new identity propelled her into the leadership role in what was to become an annual event—the antiabortion march on the Capitol, the so-called March for Life.

She lived alone in a comfortable townhouse on Sixth Street southeast, just a few blocks from the Capitol. In the fall of 1973 she was approached by some right-to-lifers from New York, veterans of battles against the

legislature and Governor Nelson Rockefeller, who told her
that they wanted to commemorate January 22, 1974, the
first anniversary of the infamous Supreme Court decision,
with a march. They needed a headquarters in Washington,
they said; could they possibly use her place? Nellie Gray
said yes, they could. So they held a series of meetings in
her dining room, and decided to bring in people from all
over the country to participate in the march. They needed
a Washington phone number, they said; could they possibly use hers? She said yes. Then they said they needed a
Washington mailing address. She said yes, they could use
her address as well. She has been running the march ever
since.

That first year, about six thousand marchers descended
on the Capitol to show their strength and to lobby senators,
congressmen, their staffs, and other government employees.
As a one-shot lobbying effort, it was spectacular. But congressmen have a way of disappearing, of being in conference
or out of town, when such events take place. When the
marchers dispersed, only Nellie Gray was left to remind
elected officials that abortion was wrong. She registered as
a full-time lobbyist, one of the first right-to-lifers to do so.
Since 1974, that is the way Nellie Gray has spent her life—
organizing the annual march, and lobbying tirelessly (although in the summer of 1980 Dr. Jack Willke said she was
"pretty well down the list as far as effectiveness is concerned").

In the course of her work she has made many friends.
The basement of her townhouse is a maze of filing cabinets
containing the names and addresses of marchers in every
state. She is constantly on the phone, chatting with friends

in the movement. She gives the impression of a woman who enjoys her work. And yet, she says this is not entirely true.

The organizers of the original march chose the red rose as their emblem. Every January 22, the marchers distribute thousands of roses to their targets on Capitol Hill. The rose was chosen for two reasons, the first of which was financial; according to the 1980 March for Life official program, orders for roses at $2 each "fund the March for Life on a year-by-year basis . . ." But the rose was also chosen for its symbolic value. "The red rose," says the program, has been "long emblematic of beauty and martyrdom." It is its evocation of martyrdom that makes the rose a fitting symbol for Nellie Gray; in fact, part of the reason she calls for a Nuremberg-like trial of those who support abortion is the notion that she and her colleagues have been compelled to work in the antiabortion effort. "You cannot force people such as myself to turn our lives over for eight or nine years trying to defend babies that the government should be defending, and then everybody just walk away from it and say, 'Well, isn't that nice, now we have a constitutional amendment.'" If Nellie Gray chooses to engage in full-time right-to-life work (no one, of course, forced her into it), and if, further, Nellie Gray chooses to view her right-to-life work as an inconvenience, then the people who Nellie Gray believes forced her to suffer this inconvenience must be made accountable.

"I have read some amusing and fanciful fictionalized accounts of my background," says Dr. Mildred Faye Jefferson, smiling a brilliant, controlled smile. "But they don't bear very much relationship to the truth." The reason for this is probably that Dr. Jefferson is extremely stingy with information about herself, particularly with regard to dates. But according to the registrar's office at Texas College in Tyler, Texas, she was born on April 6, 1927, in the town of Carthage, in East Texas, and she graduated from Texas College in 1945, at the tender age of eighteen. Jefferson herself acknowledges that she is the only progeny of a Methodist preacher and a schoolteacher. "My family never had any money as such," she says, "but they represented the top of the limited social structure in which we lived." Her mother's family—the name was Roberts—had land; the first school Mildred attended was on land donated by the Robertses, as was the first church.

She left Texas after graduating from college, and set out for Boston to become a doctor. She succeeded; after taking premed courses at Tufts University, she moved on to Harvard Medical School, from which she received her M.D. in 1951. She did postgraduate work at Tufts, and interned at Boston City Hospital. It was not until much later that she became interested in the abortion issue.

In 1970, at the annual convention of the American Medical Association, a resolution was offered that would considerably soften the AMA's position on abortion. It held that doctors would not be considered unethical for performing whatever abortions were legal under a given state's laws. Dr. Jefferson learned of this resolution when a friend, a fellow doctor, asked her to sign a petition protesting it. She did. When the resolution passed anyway, she and other like-minded citizens in Massachusetts formed an educational organization called the Value of Life

Committee. The members thought that simply by making information available to those who requested it, they would be able to counter the movement to liberalize the state's abortion laws.

But on November 7, 1972—election day—something happened to shake that assumption: citizens in 17 Massachusetts communities approved a nonbinding referendum in favor of more liberal abortion laws. It became clear to Jefferson and her colleagues that as an educational organization, the Value of Life Committee was too passive; they decided to enter more directly into the political arena. They set about to find and organize independent pro-life groups into a coalition. This assemblage eventually became Massachusetts Citizens for Life, which became incorporated in January 1973, shortly before the Supreme Court handed down *Roe* v. *Wade* and *Doe* v. *Bolton.* Jefferson was also elected to serve on the board of directors of the National Right to Life Committee.

The organization now known as the National Right to Life Committee was founded in 1973. Prior to that, another organization with the same name existed; it had been founded in 1965. The old NRLC and the new one, for the first two years of its existence, were essentially clearinghouses of information with tiny staffs; the power of the movement lay in the local organizations in every state. The new NRLC was conceived as a democratic institution with two board members from every state. These directors would be elected from boards at the state level, and representatives on the state boards (such as Massachusetts Citizens for Life) would be chosen by local right-to-life leaders, meeting in committee. In practice, many right-to-life groups have not affiliated themselves with the NRLC and thus are not represented on its board; nevertheless, the NRLC is, as its president Dr. Willke claims, the only nationally based right-to-life group with a democratically chosen board of directors.

This democratic structure was, and remains, cumbersome; with 55 directors, this is not surprising. Until 1975, there was no particular separation between the directors and the paid staff, and no distinct line of command. Thus, directors routinely involved themselves in the day-to-day operation of the organization. The results were often chaotic. In June 1975, the board elected Dr. Mildred Faye Jefferson to the presidency of the NRLC.

The first thing she attempted to do was draw a dividing line between the directors and the operating staff. She would be the only boss the staff had to worry about. This, of course, enhanced her own power, and there were those on the board who resented this. But Jefferson was elected to two additional one-year terms before finally being defeated by a Phoenix, Arizona, physician, Dr. Carolyn Gerster, in 1978. The NRLC needed Jefferson, because she brought it, and the movement in general, something it sought desperately: a clear image independent of the Catholic Church. The power in the church for nearly two thousand years had been exclusively male; the most powerful officer of the NRLC was now a female. The church power structure was almost exclusively white; the NRLC president was black. And of course, Mildred Jefferson was not a Catholic.

It is likely that when she assumed the presidency, she brought with her a small reserve of national recognition;

for five months prior to her appointment she had been involved in the manslaughter trial of Dr. Kenneth C. Edelin. In October 1973, Dr. Edelin performed a second-trimester therapeutic abortion on a Boston teenager at Boston City Hospital. He used a standard procedure in such late cases—a hysterotomy, which is similar to a Caesarean section. In April 1974, Edelin was indicted for causing the death of the fetus after it was removed from the mother (although there would be conflicting testimony about whether the fetus actually drew a breath—or, indeed, was capable of drawing a breath—outside the mother's body). The trial began in Boston in January 1975, and Dr. Jefferson—by this time well-known locally as an antiabortion crusader—was granted the status of expert witness.

No one questioned the legality of the abortion performed by Dr. Edelin. The prosecution was based on the notion that he had not done everything in his power to resuscitate the fetus once it had been removed. In her testimony, Jefferson said a fetus becomes a baby when the placenta is severed—the implication being that Edelin should have done something to save it. Edelin and his attorney, William P. Homans, Jr., contended there was nothing to be done; the fetus "never drew breath," Homans said.

At the close of the trial, when Judge James P. McGuire delivered his charge to the jury, Edelin and Homans believed a verdict of innocent was inevitable, for the judge said a conviction was possible only if the fetus were, in fact, a person, and then only if the jury were convinced beyond a reasonable doubt that Edelin had shown wanton and reckless conduct. But when the jury returned and the judge asked for a verdict, the foreman, Vincent Shea, *shouted* the word "Guilty"; the judge subsequently failed to issue the traditional word of thanks to the jury following the close of a trial.

The extent to which Dr. Jefferson's testimony influenced the jury is not clear, but there were other factors that Edelin contended weighed heavily in the verdict. To begin with, ten of the twelve jurors were Catholic. In addition, racial tension in Boston was high due to forced busing in the school system; Edelin was black and the jury was all white. "It was a witch hunt," he commented after the verdict had been delivered. Had the conviction stood, of course, very few doctors subsequently would have risked performing anything but first-trimester abortions. In December 1976, however, the Massachusetts Supreme Judicial Court overturned the conviction.

Four years after the trial, the *Boston Globe* disclosed that, in addition to testifying against Edelin, Dr. Jefferson had played another role in the controversy. After Edelin's indictment, the faculty at the Boston University Medical School, which runs Boston City Hospital, voted to provide Edelin with financial support for his legal fees. Jefferson, a member of the B.U. Medical School faculty, announced that she would take legal action to block any such aid. She succeeded in blocking any formal offer of assistance. (In 1979, Edelin joined Dr. Jefferson on the B.U. faculty.)

During her three years as president of the National Right to Life Committee Mildred Jefferson was a highly visible figure, traveling across the country, making speeches and debating. (Her most frequent opponent was the right-to-life movement's bête noire, Bill Baird.) In her speeches she usually stressed the view that abortion was a means of controlling or eliminating the poor. In 1977 she wrote:

> Government funding of abortion is a cruel hoax perpetrated by those social planners in and out of government who have mounted a class war against the poor. They believe that to be poor is to be genetically inferior. They also believe that providing help for the poor that would lead them to self-sufficiency is futile and unduly costly. They use the money intended to help the poor to get rid of the poor by abortion, sterilization, or any other measures which might gain legal acceptance. The genocidal aspects are incidental: minority racial groups make up a disproportionately large share of "the poor." They naturally become the largest numbers of the expendable.[1]

She reserved much of her wrath for members of her own race who were instrumental in securing funding for abortions for the poor. She was infuriated when Supreme Court Justice Thurgood Marshall voted in favor of states and municipal governments being required to pay for abortions. She wrote of Marshall:

> This nation must be appalled that one whose early life was spent fighting for racial justice cannot recognize that he has become unjust to the poor of all races. He may have saved one race from the threat of lynchings in the southern swamps, but by condoning the government-funded abortion of the poor, he is condemning a people to extinction.[2]

Her initial premise—that "social planners" would rather eliminate the poor than spend money to help them—seems

far-fetched, since most of the government officials who
supported funding for abortion also supported a panoply
of costly social programs, while most who opposed abortion
funding also opposed the social programs. The liberal philosophy was to give the poor pregnant woman the means
to make a choice: she could choose abortion, financed by
the government, or motherhood; if she chose the latter she
would be sustained by Medicaid, food stamps, government-
financed day-care programs, and other aid. The conservative philosophy was to deny the woman the opportunity
to have an abortion, while at the same time voting against
the social programs from which she would benefit when
forced to carry the pregnancy to term. Dr. Jefferson's
reasoning may have arisen from her tendency—shared by
most in the right-to-life movement—to find no distinction
between abortion by choice and *mandatory* abortion.
Asked about this in a 1980 interview, she responded with
the extraordinary statement that "once you do something
voluntarily, you have no grounds to object if it is required."
Thus, in her mind, Justice Marshall and those who shared
his views were not simply advocating freedom of choice
for poor women, but were paving the way for a program
that might some day force poor women to abort their
pregnancies, whether they wanted to or not.

CHAPTER 7

"THOU SHALT NOT KILL ZYGOTES"

For the most part, fundamentalist Protestants did not join the right-to-life movement until the late 1970s. This is not because the fundamentalists did not oppose abortion before that time, but because it was only in the late seventies that they became politically active in significant numbers. Prior to that time there were scattered efforts by fundamentalist clergymen to pressure public school systems and libraries into banning certain books, just as there were local campaigns to ban sex education and pornography and to reinstitute school prayer, but for the most part, preachers counseled against involvement in the world at large. In 1965 a preacher in Lynchburg, Virginia, named Jerry Falwell expressed this view: "We are not told to wage wars against bootleggers, liquor stores, gamblers, murderers, prostitutes, racketeers, prejudiced persons or institutions, or any other existing evil as such. Our ministry is not reformation but transformation. The gospel does not clean up the outside but rather regenerates the inside . . ."[1] It was not until much later that Falwell repudiated this view as false prophecy.

But five years before Jerry Falwell became a national political power, one fundamentalist Christian—a layman, not a preacher—began crusading against abortion, and his impact has been significant.

In 1950, when he met the woman who would become his wife, Murray Norris was a twenty-two-year-old reporter for the *Sacramento Bee*. He was also, by his own admission, a humanist; he had attended several colleges, and had fallen under the spell of professors who shed doubt on the existence of God, and who favored such things as birth control as an answer to population growth. (He heard later, secondhand, that at least a few of these professors had been seen attending Communist Party cell meetings.) He did believe in God, but it was a popcorn God, what he now calls a "gimme God" ("Y'know, 'Gimme what I want'?"). He had dated hundreds of women, but was skeptical about getting married, because divorce ran in his family. His parents were divorced, as were his mother's parents and his father's parents. What chance had he?

Beth was an underwriter for an insurance company in Sacramento when they met. She was also sickly; she was taking medication for anemia, and told Murray she would never be able to have children. One night, after he had left her in his car for several hours while he took pictures of a flood for the *Bee*, she told him she loved him. Jarred by this bit of information, he took the matter up with the Lord the next time he was alone. In a sweet voice, like that of a loving father, the Lord said, "Marry her."

Murray Norris answered, "But she can't have any kids."

"Marry her," God repeated.

Murray Norris thought he was dealing with a gimme

God, so he asked for a fully paid-for house as a sign that He meant what He said. God delivered; Murray's mother gave him $5,500, enough to buy a three-bedroom house and five acres. So he married Beth. By the time he left the newspaper business twenty-two years later to crusade full-time against abortion, pornography, sex education, and satanism, she had borne him thirteen children. He had wanted twelve and considered the thirteenth an extra blessing.

That was the only time God spoke to Murray Norris directly. But from time to time, God has given him signs that have guided his life. In the middle fifties, for example, he went to law school at night; he took the California bar exam in 1957. The passing grade was 70; he scored 67½. He took this as a divine mandate that he was not to practice law. This was fine with him, anyway; he had decided he had no taste for corporate law, and as for something civic-minded—like being a public defender—"Well, many of the people that have been poor, God love 'em, have not learned to be peaceful poor. They are kind of obstreperous poor. They're not following what God wants." Not that Murray Norris believed the poor should be ignored—it was simply that alms for the poor should be handled by private individuals, by churches, by the local community, rather than by state and federal bureaucracies. People had reviled Herbert Hoover for saying the same thing, but Murray Norris knew Hoover had been right. Government welfare programs would destroy the country.

During the fifties and sixties Norris worked for several California newspapers, winding up in 1969 as editor of the *Fresno Guide*, which had a circulation of 84,000 and came out three times a week. In 1972, he had a disagreement with the publisher about an initiative petition on the ballot that would have sharply limited the sale of pornography in California. Norris backed the petition, but the publisher insisted that he write an editorial opposing it. Since he could not do so in good conscience, he resigned.

To stay in the newspaper business, Norris would have had to move to another town. But he liked Fresno, and was tired of moving, so he struck a deal with God: he would stay in Fresno, and begin a full-time campaign to combat the evils of the modern world. He told God he would devote his time to convincing Christians they could win through the power of prayer. He also told God that he would take it as a sign to quit if any of his kids ran into trouble with drugs or the law. The Lord was noncommital, so Norris began writing articles about fighting pornography and satanism through prayer. He worked in his bedroom, and was dependent on contributions from clergymen and other Christians for money to print and distribute his material. He also began making personal appearances before civic groups, eventually developing a series of "How to Win" seminars. His formula consists of a combination of prayer and political pressure. In one article he lists what he calls "nine winning methods": "(1) Prayer. (2) Get officials to do their job. (3) Pass new laws. (4) Petitions and letters. (5) Polls. (6) Phone campaigns. (7) Television telethons. (8) Mass mailings. (9) Exotic programs like the CLEAN campaign." (This is a reference to a citywide antipornography campaign in Pismo Beach, California.)

In 1973, when the Supreme Court legalized abortion, Norris found a new focus. Within a few weeks, a local pastor agreed to pay for 10,000 copies of an antiabortion newspaper, and Norris put out the first copy of *Right to Life News*. The lead story featured a letter from Governor Ronald Reagan in which Reagan apologized for signing California's liberal abortion law in 1967. (*Right to Life News*, still published several times a year, is not to be confused with the official newsletter of the National Right to Life Committee, which is called *National Right to Life News*.)

Shortly after putting out the first *Right to Life News*, he decided that he needed something to reach pregnant teenage girls, something to get across the serious nature of abortion. He discussed some ideas with a professional cartoonist named Kevin Barrett; the result was Norris's favorite publication—a 24-page cartoon book entitled "Who Killed Junior?" In a simplistic manner, the drawings traced the growth of a fertilized egg in the womb. By the sixth week "Junior" is a fully formed baby, standing up and smiling; by the eleventh week he is running in place and has a decent command of colloquial English; he is thinking, "Time for me to get going soon." At three months, Junior has his hand cupped to his ear, listening in alarm. The caption says, "His mother and her doctor are already discussing how to kill him." Then follow four panels in which the basic methods of abortion are listed. In the first, Junior screams as a vacuum cleaner sucks him out of the womb (the vacuum suction method). In the second, Junior screams as a knife slices him to pieces (dilation and curettage). In the third, Junior screams as a hand plucks him from the womb (hysterotomy). And in the fourth, Junior screams as a hypodermic needle injects saline solution into the womb (salting out). The next panel shows a fully formed baby with a knife through it, and says, "If you are a Teenage Girl—You Need to Know Abortion Means Killing a Human Being. It is Not Like a Tonsil Operation."

By presenting "Junior" as a fully conscious individual with the intellectual capacity of, perhaps, a five-year-old, the booklet works to create enormous guilt feelings in any teenager contemplating abortion. The book ends with a warning: "If you find yourself in trouble over a pregnancy —never think that abortion is an easy way out. There are unscrupulous doctors who will tell you it is, but they are more concerned with your money than your life or the life of your baby." This is consistent with a basic tenet of the right-to-life movement; that *no* doctor who performs abortions is interested in anything but the bottom line. (An exception is sometimes made for the most prolific abortionist of all, Dr. Bernard Nathanson; now that he is a convert, it is explained that his motives were humane, but his thinking was misguided.) By 1980, four million copies of "Who Killed Junior?" had been printed and distributed to junior high and high school students across the country.

Murray Norris knows "Junior" has been effective; he knows because he keeps track. In 1976, he established a "National Pregnancy Hotline"—at first, nothing more than two WATS telephones in his bedroom. He has the phone numbers printed on the back covers of new editions of "Junior"; each new distribution of "Junior" results in a flurry of calls. The callers are referred to organizations or individuals in their communities who are willing to help see them through the pregnancies. Based on the number of booklets distributed and the number of calls the hotline receives, Norris estimates that in most of the nation, one abortion is averted for every one hundred "Juniors" distributed. In the South, the ratio jumps to three fetuses saved for every one hundred "Juniors." Norris says he cannot explain this discrepancy.

In 1974 he moved his printing operation out of his bedroom, first to an office in a downtown shopping center, then to a building across the street from a junkyard and a barrel factory in the town of Clovis, just outside Fresno. In that building Murray Norris has address plates for more than 200,000 individuals and organizations. In 1976 he published more than one hundred different pieces of literature, more than eight million copies altogether. It was his peak year, but he continues to churn out a high volume of material. In an ecumenical gesture, he contracts out some of his printing work to Elasah Drogin's Catholics United for Life; he also serves on its board of advisers. The commune in Coarsegold is less than an hour's drive north of Fresno.

Murray Norris and other fundamentalists crusading against abortion rarely appear troubled by the fact that the Bible contains no specific injunction against abortion. It is an issue which crops up occasionally, however, and in 1976 a fundamentalist preacher wrote a book in which he attempted to deal with it.

The Reverend Donald Shoemaker, pastor of the Los Altos Brethren Church in Long Beach, California, says in his book, *Abortion, The Bible, and the Christian,* "I acknowledge the personhood of the unborn at every stage of the prenatal period." Still, Shoemaker is faced with the

problem of finding in Scripture something that will justify
the application of the Sixth Commandment—"You shall
not commit murder"—to the abortionist. To do this, he
strings together a series of passages which show (1) that
childbearing is blessed ("Behold, children are a gift of the
Lord; The fruit of the womb is reward" Psalm 127:3) and
(2) that the Lord values the unborn as much as He values
the born. Here he uses a passage from the 139th Psalm
which, in various translations, is probably the most frequently quoted bit of Scripture among right-to-lifers:

> For Thou didst form my inward parts;
> Thou didst weave me in my mother's womb.
> I will give thanks to Thee, for I am fearfully
> and wonderfully made;
> Wonderful are Thy works,
> And my soul knows it very well.
> My frame was not hidden from Thee,
> When I was made in secret,
> And skillfully wrought in the depths of the earth.
> Thine eyes have seen my unformed substance;
> And in Thy book they were all written,
> The days that were ordained from me,
> When as yet there was no one of them.

"This fascinating psalm contains Scripture's most complete
account of prenatal development," Shoemaker writes, correctly. And yet it would seem that the weaving analogy
(other translations use the word "knit") gives support to
those who would say that the fetus is not, in fact, a person
until it is born—just as a sweater is not a sweater until the
knitting or weaving of it is done. It is certainly an arguable
point, and not the clear mandate from God that Shoemaker is seeking.

Shoemaker and others who depend on the Bible for their case against abortion studiously ignore massive evidence that, at best, God bestowed his blessings on only some, not all, fetuses. When God went into one of his genocidal rages, very few people were safe, and God apparently had no compunction about killing the unborn along with their parents. Given the nature of the activities in Sodom and Gomorrah just before God destroyed those cities, it is reasonable to assume that an unusually high percentage of women, married or not, were pregnant. And there is no evidence of any lack of fecundity just prior to the Great Flood. We are told that God punished only the wicked, and right-to-lifers tell us there is no such thing as a wicked fetus; even if the mother is wicked, the fetus is innocent. If God was not punishing the fetuses He killed, there can be but one explanation: He simply did not regard them as persons.

In his book, Shoemaker offers a justification for his opposition to abortion:

As a Christian, I am alarmed by the extent to which recent trends related to permissive abortion are affecting our value system. Whereas Scripture places a premium on the joys of the home, the worth of child-bearing and love for kin, we see these coming out second-best to the pursuit of career, the overplayed population explosion (at least in America), and a materialism which can seemingly afford almost everything except another child.

Such a statement represented the sentiments of a political phenomenon which was just gathering force in 1976—the so-called pro-family movement.

The pro-family movement evolved largely as a protest

against the values represented by the feminist movement. In November 1977, when thousands of women gathered in Houston to climax International Women's Year, another large group of people convened for a "pro-family rally" in the Astrodome only a few miles away. There, people carried signs which said, "E.R.A. Is a Turkey," "God Made Adam and Eve, Not Adam and Steve," and "IWY—International Witches Year." Speakers at this rally included Dr. Mildred Jefferson, Nellie Gray, and Phyllis Schlafly, head of Stop ERA, as well as Representative Robert K. Dornan, the California Republican who cosponsored a no-exceptions version of the human life amendment.

Two and a half years later, these conferences in Houston were paralleled by a pair of events in Southern California. In 1980, the administration of President Jimmy Carter sponsored a series of meetings collectively titled the White House Conference on Families. The traditional nuclear family was represented at these meetings, but so were single-parent families, families without children, families similar to the nuclear family except that the parents are not married, and homosexual couples of both sexes. To the segment of the American population which called itself pro-family, this was nothing short of sacrilege. To them, the very term "families" was loaded; there was, in fact, only one grouping of people that could be called a family, and this grouping included a breadwinning, churchgoing father, a housekeeping, churchgoing mother, and upward of two clean, obedient churchgoing children. In fact Ed McAteer, head of an organization called the Religious Round Table, had promulgated a set of principles against which any conglomeration of people wishing to call themselves a family might be tested. A sampling:

Family. A family consists of persons who are related by blood, marriage, or adoption. A family is not a commune, or a homosexual liaison, or extramarital liaison. Efforts to legitimize that kind of illegitimate relationship insult traditional families.

Primacy of Family. The strength and stability of families determine the vitality and moral life of society. The most important function of the family is the rearing and character formation of children, a function it was uniquely created to perform, and for which no remotely adequate substitute has been found.

Education. Parents have the primary right and responsibility to educate children according to the philosophy of their choice without government interference or financial penalty. (Parents should have equitable access to private schools for their children's education, without suffering grave, undue hardship financially. In order for that to be possible, schools must not be harassed by the government, nor may students from private schools be discriminated against by policy or law.)

Parental Rights. God has given parents the right and responsibility to rear and form the character of their children in accordance with His laws. (The pro-family coalition is unalterably opposed to government policies and judicial decisions which permit or promote government-funded "services" of counseling, contraception, and abortion to minor children without parental knowledge and consent. The pro-family movement opposes federal funding of pornographic sex-education materials promoted by Planned Parenthood as a "cure" for teenage pregnancies.)[2]

The last session of Jimmy Carter's Conference on Families took place the weekend of July 12–13 in Los Angeles. On July 12, in nearby Long Beach, a counter-convention was held to protest it. This gathering was called America's Pro-Family Conference. A comparison of the program of this event and the speaker's roster at the 1977 pro-family rally in Houston reveals the extent to which the movement had evolved into a theo/political force during the intervening 32 months.

Mildred Jefferson spoke at both rallies, as did Phyllis Schlafly. But now they were joined by influential political figures, notably Howard Phillips, head of the Conservative Caucus, and Senator Jesse Helms of North Carolina. (Ronald Reagan was on the program as well, but sent his regrets. The Republican Convention which would nominate him for President was to begin two days later, and he found it necessary to devote his full attention to it.) In addition, three fundamentalist preachers with national constituencies were on hand: Bill Bright, president of Campus Crusade for Christ International, Jerry Falwell, head of the Moral Majority, and the Reverend Tim LaHaye, of El Cajon, California, the master of ceremonies.

LaHaye, a lean and handsome man with an angular face, slick, dark hair, and long sideburns, is one of the most prominent theoreticians of the pro-family movement. His educational background is as follows: B.A., Bob Jones University, 1950; D.D., Bob Jones University, 1962; D. Min., Western Conservative Baptist Theological Seminary, 1977. In the summer of 1980, he was head of an organization called Californians for a Biblical Morality. He was also chancellor of Christian Heritage College in El Cajon, a city ten miles east of San Diego in the desert country. Christian Heritage College has a single mission: to promote the Biblical theory of creation. The 500 students who attend classes on the 32-acre campus—as well as an additional 2,500 students who attend grades one through twelve in the schools that make up the Christian Unified School District, with which the college is associated—know that ten thousand years ago God created the Earth, and He created all the animals and plants in their present form, and He created Man; these students also know that evolution is a discredited theory.

In 1980, the bookstore at Christian Heritage College was housed in cramped, temporary quarters, which necessarily limited the number of volumes on display. One pair of authors, however, was amply represented: Dr. Tim LaHaye and his wife, Beverly. Among the titles on sale were these: *The Beginning of the End*, by Tim LaHaye; *Revelation (Illustrated and Made Plain)* by Tim LaHaye; *How to Win over Depression*, by Tim LaHaye; *The Spirit-controlled Woman*, by Beverly LaHaye; *Spirit-controlled Family Living*, by Beverly and Tim LaHaye; *How to Develop Your Child's Temperament*, by Beverly LaHaye; *How to be Happy* Though *Married*, by Tim LaHaye; *The Act of Marriage—the Beauty of Sexual Love*, by Tim and Beverly LaHaye; *The Unhappy Gays*, by Tim LaHaye; and *The Battle of the Mind*, by Tim LaHaye. (LaHaye also markets the LaHaye Temperament Analysis Test, which, according to a brochure, will "identify your primary and secondary temperament" and "provide you with a list of your spiritual gifts, in order of their priority." The test is available by mail at $19.95 per copy, unless accompanied

by a $5 discount certificate; the buyer is told to complete
the form, send it in, and the test "will then be scored,
analyzed, and a personal evaluation prepared." Then,
"Your personal 13 to 15 page evaluation letter from Dr.
Tim LaHaye will be permanently bound in a vinyl-leather
portfolio and returned to you by mail.")

In his book *The Battle of the Mind*, LaHaye presents
his vision of the intellectual history of Western civilization.
It is startling in that he severely criticizes periods of intellectual ferment (which he equates with humanism) while
appearing much more comfortable with periods of stagna-
tion. For example, we are accustomed to thinking of
ancient Greece as a marvelous island of rational thought in
a world of mysticism and barbarism, but LaHaye condemns
Greek thinkers for being "the first to systematically lay
out the philosophy of humanism that Paul described as the
wisdom of man." LaHaye quotes God in Isaiah 55:8:
"'For my thoughts are not your thoughts, neither are your
ways my ways, saith the Lord.'" On the other hand,
LaHaye seems pleased with the Middle Ages: ". . . so effective did Christianity become in influencing the thought of
Western man for over 1,200 years that, from the death of
Christ until the twelfth century, little humanistic thinking
is found." But then, in the thirteenth century, the seeds
for humanism again found fertile ground—in the person of
Thomas Aquinas, who "opened the door for free-thinking
educators to gradually implant more of the wisdom of
man, as they discarded the wisdom of God." To LaHaye,
the Renaissance was merely the period "which gave birth
to modern humanism," and "The Renaissance obsession

with nude 'art forms' was the forerunner of the modern humanist's demand for pornography in the name of freedom." (LaHaye cites Michelangelo's *David* as the prime example.) According to LaHaye, "The two men who wield the greatest influence upon the humanistic ideals, morals, and philosophy of today's college students are the French skeptics Voltaire and Rousseau. Both were trained in Jesuit colleges, yet both rejected anything supernatural and adopted an ethically amoral code."

At every step, LaHaye accurately emphasizes the contrast between the absolutism of what he calls "Christian thought" and the relativism inherent in humanist thought. Of course he prefers the former. He sums up:

> Simply defined, humanism is man's attempt to solve his problems independently of God. Since moral conditions have become worse and worse in direct proportion to humanism's influence, which has moved our country from a biblically based society to an amoral "democratic" society during the past forty years, one would think that humanists would realize the futility of their position. To the contrary, they treacherously refuse to face the reality of their failures, blaming them instead on traditional religion or ignorance or capitalism or religious superstitions.

It was for this reason that Tim LaHaye told the audience at America's Pro-Family Conference in Long Beach in July 1980 that "a humanist is not fit to be a governor, a politician, a leader, or an educator in the United States of America." Humanists, he added magnanimously, "should be permitted to live here, but by no stretch of the imagination should we pay their salaries with our taxes so they can destroy us."

A short time after LaHaye spoke at the conference, Howard Phillips, head of the Conservative Caucus, explained in religious terms why conservatives should be elected to lead the country. Phillips said, "The liberals believe that the state is God. The libertarians believe that Man is God. And the conservatives, at least those to whose doctrines I subscribe, believe that God is God." This was greeted with prolonged applause. Then Phillips added, "When your rights come from government they are very alienable. Only when these rights are God-given rights are those rights secure."

Later on in the program, the Reverend Bill Bright, president of Campus Crusade for Christ International, explained to the conservative, God-fearing audience the significance of the abortion issue. He delivered a sermon in which he said that abortion was simply the latest, and most severe, in a series of plagues God had inflicted on America in retaliation for the Supreme Court's 1963 decision banning mandatory prayer sessions in public schools. Bright's reasoning went like this:

> . . . now the schools where God had been honored had been closed to God . . . Almost within a matter of days, President John F. Kennedy was assassinated . . . then the war in Vietnam accelerated . . . the drug culture swept millions of our young people into the drug scene. These are plagues, in my opinion. And God was trying to get our attention but we still didn't listen to Him . . .
>
> And so we kept on our materialistic way, lethargic, and indifferent to the ways of God, increasingly. And

He sent more plagues. The youth revolution threatened to overthrow our government. Senator Kennedy was assassinated. Martin Luther King was assassinated. The homes of America began to disintegrate, until one out of every two marriages ended in divorce. We still didn't listen to God. He was trying to get our attention. And then there developed an epidemic of drug addiction. An epidemic of alcoholism. An epidemic of teenage pregnancy . . . an epidemic of venereal disease. And then the Supreme Court legalized murder. And some ten million people, unborn babies, have been destroyed . . .

Abortion, said Bright, was the worst plague God had visited on America *so far*, but unless Americans re-enthroned Him in a hurry, they would be in for economic collapse, followed by a takeover by the Russians.

Bright's audience responded enthusiastically. It did not seem strange to anyone that God would use the Supreme Court as an instrument to avenge an act of the Supreme Court. Perhaps it was logical.

By 1980 fundamentalist preachers around the country had renounced their previous noninvolvement in politics. In a pamphlet entitled "Christians in Government: What the Bible Says," the Reverend Jerry Falwell had written:

God intended for Christians to be the "salt of the world," to have a preserving influence on our nation, holding it back from moral spoilage and decay. Throughout history, God has raised up individuals to represent Him in the political arena. Today, we must stand up for God in our democratic republic, using voice He granted us. The ungodly cannot be expected to elect righteous officials and to enact legislation based on God's laws. But

God's people can make the difference in this nation if they are willing to pay the price of personal involvement.

God's people apparently were willing to pay the price. Thus, during the last years of the seventies and the beginning of the eighties fundamentalist Protestants were able to make common cause with an unlikely ally, the Catholic Church. And to this union came a third, crucial element: a born-again Republican Party.

CHAPTER 8

THE NEW RIGHT TAKES OVER THE GRAND OLD PARTY

On the evening of July 18, 1980, Dr. Jack C. Willke returned to his home in Finneytown, Ohio, a suburb of Cincinnati, after a week at the Republican National Convention in Detroit. He retired briefly to the master bedroom of the split-level brick house, took off his three-piece gray suit, put on a white sports shirt and blue shorts, and joined his wife, Barbara, on the patio for a steak cookout. Between bites, he talked about George Bush.

On February 15, Ronald Reagan had pledged that his running mate, whoever it might be, would share Reagan's antiabortion beliefs. In a telegram to Father Charles Fiore —who was, by now, chairman of an organization called the National Pro-Life Political Action Committee—Reagan said:

> My strong position that protection of the unborn is a major issue facing our nation is well known to your movement. Additionally, I have stated that it is my intention to have a vice-presidential running-mate whose beliefs are consistent with my major principles, and who would support and carry out my policies and programs.

To the right-to-life movement, this meant that Reagan would choose, perhaps, Representative Jack Kemp, or Senator Richard Lugar, Senator Paul Laxalt, or Senator Richard Schweiker—all of whom they would have been satisfied with—or Representative Henry Hyde or Senator Jesse Helms—two they would have been ecstatic about. But George Bush simply would not do; in fact, Father Fiore had labeled Bush's record on abortion "atrocious." Yet now, following Reagan's selection of Bush, Dr. Willke seemed pleased.

This is because only two days earlier, it had seemed a certainty that Ronald Reagan would choose as his running mate former President Gerald R. Ford. Reagan and Ford had been negotiating for a week, and it was clear that Ford would not accept the nomination for vice president unless he were given specific areas of responsibility that would make him the most powerful vice president in history. And although Ford had repeatedly expressed personal opposition to abortion, he was, in the eyes of right-to-life leaders, emphatically proabortion. When, during an interview, Walter Cronkite asked Ford whether there was anything in the 1980 Republican Party platform with which he disagreed, Ford singled out planks supporting a human life amendment and the selection of federal judges based on their antiabortion views. The choice of Ford would have been a clear repudiation of the right-to-life movement.

So when Reagan announced that the deal with Ford had fallen through, and the choice was Bush, Jack Willke was relieved and happy, "because Bush was not going to be a co-president. He was going to be a nobody." In addition, Bush had announced that he would "enthusiastically support" the entire Republican platform.

Still, Willke did not entirely accept Bush. "You know, there are *nuances,*" he said, and he recounted a Bush press conference he had seen on television following the nomination. "They asked him about [abortion], one lady did. And the words he used were not *quite* as direct as the ones he'd used the night before . . . He said, 'Now look.' He said it almost impatiently, that sort of a tone of voice. He said, 'I have said, and this I mean, that I oppose abortion, and I am for equal rights for women.' And he said, 'I don't think we should get lost in a lot of . . .' What he meant was, a lot of minutiae or details or something of that sort . . . But if you take the exact words he said that time, 'I oppose abortion,' well, Kennedy could say that."

Willke and the rest of the movement decided to wait and see about George Bush. There was always the possibility that he would revert to his old proabortion ways. But transcending that, there was the fact that George Bush was not the kind of Republican the movement was entirely comfortable with. Although he had moved from Connecticut to Texas, he still looked and sounded like the eastern prep school kid he had been. His political heritage was from the Rockefeller wing of the party, not the Reagan wing. And the Republicans whom right-to-lifers admired were extremely rough on elitism—men like Jesse Helms, and Henry J. Hyde.

In 1976, Hyde and another young Republican congressman, Representative Robert Bauman of Maryland, wrote an amendment to an appropriations bill in an effort to prohibit federal funding of abortions unless the mother's life were in danger. Hyde introduced the amendment, which passed both the House and Senate that year, and in every subsequent year (although sometimes with slightly less restrictive language); although Henry Hyde did not author all of these bills, the measure always carried his name. (The federal government continued to fund abortions for poor women for four years while a series of court challenges took place; in the summer of 1980, the U.S. Supreme Court ruled, 5–4, that the Hyde Amendment was constitutional, and the funding was halted.)

Henry Hyde was born in Chicago on April 18, 1924. His father was English, his mother Irish, and both were Democrats. Henry went to Georgetown University on a basketball scholarship, then served as an officer in the Navy from 1944 to 1946. After the war, he went to Loyola University Law School, and got his degree in 1949. By this time he was already leaning away from the Democratic Party.

The last Democratic candidate for President he supported was President Harry Truman, in 1948. Truman was a haberdasher from Missouri, while the Republican nominee was Thomas E. Dewey, a symbol of the eastern establishment. In 1952, the situation changed drastically. The Democratic nominee this time was Adlai E. Stevenson, a divorced intellectual to the left of Truman on the political spectrum. Stevenson looked, and talked, like a college professor. The Republican nominee was an all-American war hero from Kansas, General Dwight D. Eisenhower. Hyde decided the Democrats had moved too far left, and supported Eisenhower. Then, like other prominent conservatives—Ronald Reagan, Jesse Helms, and Strom Thurmond—Hyde formally abandoned the Democratic Party, and registered as a Republican. After serving four terms in the Illinois Legislature he ran for Congress in 1974 and won. Following the enactment of the Hyde Amendment. Henry Hyde quickly became the speaker most in demand at right-to-life conventions and banquets. His rhetoric at these events owes much to two politicians who had considerable success as anti-elitists in the late 1960s: former Alabama Governor George C. Wallace and former Vice President Spiro T. Agnew. Wallace, a symbol of southern resistance to the civil rights movement, relied heavily on the term "pointy-headed professors" in his run for the presidency in 1968, while Agnew, who once said, "If you've seen one ghetto, you've seen them all," sneered at "effete intellectual snobs." This rhetoric was always critical of people who would be identified today as secular humanists—that is; proponents of forced busing, sex education, arms control, the Equal Rights Amendment, and social welfare programs. It was pseudo-populist talk, meant to imply a return of power to "the people"—but not *all* the people; it did not resonate among traditional Republicans, but among a crucial segment of Franklin Roosevelt's New Deal coalition—white middle- and lower-middle-class people who felt squeezed by "welfare cheats" from below and uncaring government bureaucrats from above. When an anti-busing crowd in Pontiac, Michigan, shouted "Power to the people, fuck the niggers," it was clear precisely who fit the definition of people, and who did not.

Just as Agnew and Wallace blamed "intellectuals" for everything from crime in the streets to rebellion in the classrooms, Hyde took them to task for killing fetuses. In a masterful speech to the delegates of the 1980 National Right to Life Committee Convention, he said:

The opinion molders, major media, the liberal academic community, which dominate our courts and our schools —in short, the elitists of our country who wield inordinate power—are the support and strength of the pro-abortion movement. The pro-abortion appeal is most welcome among the affluent and allegedly well-educated. And I've always thought the definition of "intellectual" is one who is educated beyond his intelligence. (laughter and applause.)

The elitist character of the pro-abortion movement is revealed through its main channel of political strength —the judiciary. These judges are appointed, and truly dwell on Mt. Olympus, far removed from what some are pleased to call the political swamps; thus they are immune to the petty concerns of the people—such as abortion.

The largest pro-abortion funding comes from wealthy foundations, administered by the species of liberal I prefer to call Gucci Bolsheviks. (more laughter and applause.) The agenda of the elitist left is thus in primacy over that of the great, unwashed, vulgar masses, you and me.

The strong anti-intellectual strain is consistent with the rhetoric of Wallace and Agnew, and also ties in neatly with the antihumanist writings of Tim LaHaye. Hyde then added a new twist: those rich intellectuals, he said, *don't like children.*

Among the affluent, the satisfactions of the "Me" Generation have been given a new vitality. The problems of psychotherapy among this class indicates a self-centeredness that requires less and less time for the burdens of children. Children are the new domestic pets. And not everyone has time for the care and feeding of pets.

Meanwhile, of course, the "unenlightened poor" have an increasing birthrate, and in a representative democracy this could be a threat to the dominant elite. Abortion, therefore, is affluent America's program for the poor. Its final solution to poverty. Get rid of the people. (laughter.)

Thus, Hyde spelled out an assumption implicit in right-to-life thinking: that rich people and poor people have abortions for different reasons. The rich have abortions because children would get in the way of their hedonistic, narcissistic lifestyle, while the poor have abortions only because the rich force them to. Hyde's logic suffers from the same flaw as Mildred Jefferson's—that government-funded abortion amounts to genocide of the poor. In fact, those who favor funding for abortions also tend to favor the social programs that enable the poor to bring up their children comfortably, while those who oppose abortion tend to oppose the federal programs as well.

The transformation of the Republican Party into something in which Henry Hyde, as well as Helms, Thurmond, and Reagan could fit comfortably—not merely as right-wing extremists, but as part of the mainstream—began in 1964, when Barry Goldwater triumphed over two members of the eastern, liberal wing of the party—Nelson Rockefeller and Pennsylvania Governor William Scranton—to win the nomination for President. Conservative delegates, triumphant after years of frustration, impatiently booed Rockefeller and Scranton, but applauded enthusiastically when a newcomer to the national political scene, Ronald Reagan, made his maiden speech in support of Goldwater.

Then Goldwater himself set the tone for his disastrous campaign in a speech that seemed designed to anger, rather than soothe, the moderates in the party. "Extremism in defense of liberty is no vice; moderation in pursuit of justice is no virtue," he declared.

For the next twelve years, while the country endured the Vietnam war and Watergate, the ideological center of the Republican Party moved steadily to the right. Richard Nixon, never fully trusted by the conservatives, nevertheless helped their cause considerably by failing to support Republican candidates too liberal for his tastes. In New York, for example, liberal Republican Senator Charles Goodell accused Vice President Agnew of "dividing the country with his inflammatory rhetoric"; the Nixon Administration subsequently snubbed Goodell and gave tacit support to James Buckley, the Conservative Party candidate, who won a Senate seat in 1970 when liberals split their votes between Goodell and the Democratic candidate, Representative Richard Ottinger.

Still, in 1973, when Governor Meldrim Thomson, Jr., of New Hampshire demonstrated his disdain for the United Nations by flying the state flag at half-staff on United Nations Day, it was treated as a joke, an indication that Thomson's far-right politics were not to be taken seriously. Yet within five years a group of closely knit, powerful organizations that shared Thomson's hatred for the U.N. and anything else that hinted of "one-world government" had sprung into being. These included the National Conservative Political Action Committee (NCPAC), headed by Terry Dolan; Paul Weyrich's Committee for the Survival of a Free Congress; and the National Conservative Caucus, created by Howard Phillips, who persuaded Meldrim Thomson, Jr., to serve as chairman.

These right-wing groups were more effective than established organizations such as the John Birch Society because of their willingness and ability to appeal to uncommitted voters through single-issue politics. The key to this effort was the computerized direct-mail operation of Richard Viguerie, publisher of the *Conservative Digest* and *New Right Report*. Using sophisticated polling techniques, the New Right was able to focus on liberal politicians who appeared vulnerable in their states or districts, and to target them for defeat. Dolan's NCPAC raised money through direct-mail campaigns, and funds remaining after expenses would finance television commercials depicting the targeted liberals as big spenders, opposed to a strong national defense, and in favor of spending tax dollars to kill unborn babies. Nearly all of the ads were negative; rarely did NCPAC run positive ads about a candidate it was supporting.

But while NCPAC attacked liberals on a range of issues, other political action committees were more specialized. Among these were the National Pro-Life Political Action Committee (NPL–PAC) and the Life Amendment Political Action Committee (LAPAC).

In January 1977, Father Charles Fiore went to Washington to participate in the annual March for Life. While there he stopped in to see his congressman, Representative Henry Hyde. Fiore had been disgusted with the 1976 election campaign, in which President Ford and Jimmy Carter "did their Alphonse and Gaston act on our issue"; both said they were personally against abortion, but neither supported a human life amendment. After the election he had talked with other antiabortionists, including former Representative Harold Froelich of Wisconsin and Fran Watson, who had been active in Ellen McCormack's one-issue campaign for the Democratic nomination. He concluded that the educational approach of the National Right to Life Committee and other groups like his own Information of the Dominican Educational Association (IDEA) would not, by themselves, bring about sufficient change in the political climate to improve chances for the passage of a human life amendment. He told Hyde that he intended to form a political action committee. According to Fiore, Hyde "banged his hand down on the desk and he said, 'Father, it's a great idea. It should have been done two or three years ago. I'm all for it. Anything I can do to help, let me know.'" The result was the National Pro-Life Political Action Committee.

About the same time, Judie Brown, an employee of the National Right to Life Committee, was growing impatient with the constant political infighting at the NRLC. Dr. Mildred Jefferson, now in her third one-year term as president, had alienated a sizable group of directors, and Brown, who was the organization's public relations director, was caught in the middle. She complained to her husband, Paul, an executive with the K-Mart Corporation.

The Browns first became involved in the right-to-life movement when they were living in Seattle, Washington, in 1970, the year in which Washington liberalized its abortion laws through a referendum. During the campaign, the Browns, both Catholic, heard a sermon against abortion that disturbed them sufficiently to volunteer their time; they were among those who stood on street corners and passed out antiabortion literature with the imprint of a bloody baby's foot.

From Seattle they moved to Atlanta, where Judie Brown became heavily involved in the abortion issue—specifically with Birthright, an organization that encourages families to take in pregnant teenagers and care for them until their babies are born. The Browns were in Atlanta when the Supreme Court legalized abortion on demand.

Within the next three years they moved three more times: to North Carolina, then to Ohio, and finally to the District of Columbia. At each stop, Judie Brown immersed herself more fully in right-to-life activities; her husband joined in as well: "I'd always let them hold bake sales in front of my store, or something like this. Just do whatever I could to help out." Bake sales, in fact, fit right in with Paul Brown's philosophy regarding women; he is "totally opposed, unalterably opposed," to women's liberation. "We've come a long way since the late eighteen hundreds," he says sarcastically. "We got the women out of the factories and put them in the home. Now what are we doing today? We're putting them back in." (Brown also exhibits a discredited, if still widely held, belief about the nature of rape. When Karen Mulhauser, the attractive director of the National Abortion Rights Action League, was raped at knifepoint, Brown apparently refused to believe it—even after two men had been convicted of the crime and sent to prison. Brown was quoted in *Time* magazine and elsewhere as saying, "I hear that Karen claims she was raped. Well, let me tell you. Karen is not the most beautiful creature in the world, so when I hear her say she was raped, my response is 'You wish.'"[1] Brown later denied the quote.)

When the Browns moved to Washington, D.C., in 1976, Judie went to work as a volunteer for the National Right to Life Committee two days a week. Quickly the two days became five, and then Mildred Jefferson offered her a paid job as public relations director. She took it, but soon grew tired of the constant internecine warfare and the cumbersome structure of the NRLC.

Paul Brown says two events within the same week late in 1977 as well as his wife's complaints about the NRLC prompted him to take action on the abortion issue. During that week, newspapers carried the story of a thirty-year-old California woman who, upon dying, had been buried in her Jaguar automobile. That Sunday, in church, Brown heard a sermon in which the priest stressed over and over again that the only things of value in this world were those which a person could take with him into eternity. Brown says he was so impressed he took notes. Shortly afterward, he quit his job at K-Mart and formed the Life Amendment Political Action Committee. At first, he included among his board of directors two people who were also directors of the National Right to Life Committee, and later, for a brief while, Dr. Jack C. Willke served simultaneously on the NRLC and LAPAC boards. But by the summer of 1980 LAPAC was completely independent of, and often in disagreement with, the NRLC. By that time LAPAC's board consisted of Father Paul Marx, author of *The Death Peddlers;* Dr. Mildred Jefferson, who had been defeated for a fourth term as NRLC president in 1978; Attorney Robert L. Sassone, author of *Population Growth: The Advantages;* Sean Morton Downey, Jr., who had been a lobbyist for the NRLC but, like Judie Brown, had grown disenchanted with that organization; and Paul Brown himself. Brown was also the paid director, which gave him control over the day-to-day operations; the real power of LAPAC rested with him and with Sassone, who made the legal decisions.

From the point of view of Paul Brown and Father Charles Fiore, their Political Action Committees (PACs) had two distinct advantages over the National Right to Life Committee: they could take direct political action, and they could make decisions fast. With only a handful of board members, rather than fifty-five, they could determine policy over breakfast. There was none of the cumbersome business of having to listen to local and state boards.

Before long, significant differences in strategy and philosophy emerged between the NRLC and the two PACs. Both PACs favored a no-exceptions human life amendment, while the National Right to Life Committee favored one that allowed abortions to save the life of the mother. In the spring of 1981, when Senator Jesse Helms and Representative Henry Hyde introduced a bill intended to outlaw abortion simply by defining human life as beginning at fertilization, the NRLC supported it, while the PACs opposed it as insufficient; only an amendment to the Constitution would do. The PACs, although essentially single-issue organizations, were willing to speak out on other issues dear to the heart of the "pro-family" movement and the New Right, while the National Right to Life Committee steered clear of pornography, prayer in the schools, and homosexuality in order to build the biggest coalition possible to support a human life amendment. (Judie Brown, frustrated by these limitations, eventually left the NRLC and formed her own organization, the American Life Lobby, which occupies the same offices as her husband's LAPAC.)

The PACs, in fact, were much more willing to associate themselves with the New Right than was the NRLC. Father Fiore hired as his executive director Peter Gemma, who had been a political consultant for New Right candidates; Fiore also had a board of advisers that included Representative Henry Hyde, as well as Senator Jake Garn of Utah, a leading spokesman of the New Right. Paul Weyrich, of the Committee for Survival of a Free Congress, served as adviser to LAPAC. In June of 1980, when LAPAC Board Member Sean Morton Downey, Jr., was asked to express the main difference between LAPAC and the National Right to Life Committee, he said, "They [NRLC] are afraid of being called a tool of the New Right. We *are* a tool of the New Right, and [the New Right] is a tool of ours."

The two PACs had their first successes in the 1978 elections. Both claimed to have provided the decisive margin in the narrow, upset victories of New Right candidates Roger Jepsen and Gordon Humphrey over liberal Democratic Senators Dick Clark of Iowa and Thomas McIntyre of New Hampshire. Barely pausing for breath, Paul Brown issued a "hit list" of a dozen officeholders he planned to defeat in 1980. He did this on November 27, 1978.

Fiore followed with a hit list of his own. The lists changed from time to time as the campaign took shape; at one time or another, the targets included Senators Birch Bayh (D.-Indiana), Frank Church (D.-Idaho), John Culver

(D.-Iowa), George McGovern (D.-South Dakota), Gaylord Nelson (D.-Wisconsin), and Jacob Javits (R.-New York), all of whom were defeated, and Senators Patrick Leahy (D.-Vermont), Alan Cranston (D.-California), and Robert Packwood (R.-Oregon), who survived. The PACs also targeted a number of United States representatives—among them Father Robert Drinan, the Jesuit priest from Massachusetts who was ordered by Pope John Paul II not to run for re-election. In Paul Brown's office in the National Press Building in Washington there was a blackboard with the names of the hit list targets written on it; when Drinan announced that he would comply with the pope's order, the words "Hit by Pope" appeared next to Drinan's name on the board.

In addition to contributing money to the campaigns of candidates they supported, both PACs supplied political expertise as well. Peter Gemma was NPL-PAC's man in the field, while for LAPAC Sean Morton Downey, a self-styled lone ranger, traveled from state to state, advising right-to-life groups on tactics to defeat the targeted office-holders. Meanwhile, Paul Brown wrote letters. In one he sent to preachers in South Dakota, he wrote:

> LAPAC is a Political Action Committee targeting the defeat of legislation that is being designed for the destruction of the American family and, at the same time, sponsoring legislation that reinforces Christian family values.
>
> There are several United States Senators that have been a thorn in our side in this effort. Senator McGovern is one of these Senators. He has consistently voted in favor of anti-family legislation and is a leader in voting

for legislation on federally funded abortion.

Senator McGovern's vote in this area compromises the moral position of most Christians throughout America every pay day as federal income tax is taken out of their pay check that proportionately goes to pay for this destruction of life, which approaches two million lives per year.

But this was mild compared to Brown's first major fund-raising letter of 1981—in which he asked for help in defeating twelve senators up for re-election in 1982. At the top of the letter was a photo of a dead fetus. A caption under the fetus, printed in red ink, said "800,000,000 Slaughtered Since 1973!" To the right of the fetus was a mock poster with postage-stamp-sized pictures of the men on the hit list. "DEFEAT THE DEADLY DOZEN," the poster said: Democrats Edward M. Kennedy of Massachusetts, Robert C. Byrd of Virginia, Daniel Patrick Moynihan of New York, Lawton Chiles of Florida, Harrison Williams of New Jersey, Quentin Burdick of North Dakota, Howard Cannon of Nevada, Paul Sarbanes of Maryland, Lloyd Bentsen of Texas, and Howard Metzenbaum of Ohio, and Republicans Lowell Weicker of Connecticut and S. I. Hayakawa of California. The language in the letter was vintage Brown:

While you're reading this letter, *15 more babies will be killed* (3 a minute!)—*sucked* or *scraped* out of their mothers' wombs . . . salt poisoned or actually delivered only to be left to die. By the end of the day, 4,320 babies will have been "disposed of" by one or another of these methods—*and each one will suffer horrible pain* before their little hearts stop beating.

Fiore, too, issued a hit list early in 1981. It also included Senators Moynihan and Williams, as well as Senators George Mitchell (D.-Maine), John Chafee (R.-Rhode Island), and Representatives James Jones (D.-Oklahoma), Morris K. Udall (D.-Arizona), Stephen Neal (D.-North Carolina), Marc Lincoln Marks (R.-Pennsylvania), and Paul Findley (R.-Illinois). When Fiore's list was made public, even some of his supporters in the New Right decided that they had had enough of this sort of tactic, which could work against them easily enough if some other group were to target them as well. Henry Hyde and Jake Garn, along with Representative Robert A. Young, a Missouri Democrat, resigned in protest from NPL-PAC's advisory board.

The people who ran LAPAC, NPL-PAC, and other organizations connected with the New Right are unlike the vast majority of American political operatives in their methods of operation, their expectations, and their view of the opposition. They are unwilling to settle for the compromises that are the customary result of the give-and-take of American politics, or to acknowledge that those with opposing points of view—liberals, moderates, even traditional conservatives—are patriotic Americans who simply see things differently. To the New Right, the world is made up of us and them, good guys and bad guys—and the bad guys must be punished. In his book *The Fear Brokers*—released just after his defeat at the hands of right-winger Gordon Humphrey—former New Hampshire Senator Thomas J. McIntyre dramatically illustrated this mentality by quoting Richard Viguerie, Howard Phillips, and Paul Weyrich together:

We're going to look very carefully at the votes when all this is over and do an awful lot of punishing next election.

—Richard Viguerie

We must prove our ability to get revenge on the people who go against us.

—Howard Phillips

We are different from previous generations of conservatives. We are no longer working to preserve the status quo. We are radicals, working to overturn the present power structure of this country.

—Paul Weyrich

It is a mentality similar to that of the fundamentalist Christians, who also see the world in terms of black and white; either you're a Christian or you're a humanist, and if you say you're in the middle, that makes you a humanist. There are no shades of gray. In its absolutism it is as far removed from what was once mainstream Republican thought as are fascism and communism. But it is perfectly suited to the war against abortion.

Given the nature of the abortion issue, it is inevitable that the right-to-lifers draw the battle lines in an either/or manner. For if one chooses to view abortion as murder, then one must necessarily view abortionists as murderers, and their staffs, along with government and private agencies that support them, as accomplices, while the woman seeking the abortion is hiring someone to murder her baby. If the prevention of implantation is also murder, then the woman who wears an intrauterine device or takes low-estrogen birth control pills is a murderer, and the manufacturers of these devices and pills are accomplices. (In a world where this logic held sway, it would be entirely logical for these manufacturers to defend themselves with the slogan "IUDs don't kill zygotes—mothers do.") And if abortion is murder, then people who oppose a human life amendment—even those who approve of abortion only in cases of rape and incest—condone murder, at least in some circumstances.

In 1976 the only presidential candidate to campaign solely on an antiabortion platform was a Democrat, Ellen McCormack. But it was the Republican Party that adopted the extremist position of the right-to-life movement, writing into its platform a plank supporting "the efforts of those who seek enactment" of a human life amendment. By that time, the party was thoroughly dominated by its right wing, and it took an incumbent President, Gerald Ford, to deny Ronald Reagan the nomination. Reagan was clearly the sentimental favorite at the convention, and only the fact that many of the delegates were bound by law to support the President, who had won most of the primaries, prevented Reagan from winning. While the nomination was still in doubt, Reagan was asked to cite the clearest difference between himself and Ford on issues, and he singled out his support of the antiabortion plank.

By 1980, the ideologues of the New Right were in complete control. The party repudiated its long-standing support of the Equal Rights Amendment, and adopted strong language in support of a human life amendment, as well as a plank advocating that federal judges be appointed on the basis of their antiabortion credentials.

Reagan was endorsed by LAPAC, NPL–PAC, and major right-to-life leaders, with only one conspicuous

exception: Ellen McCormack, the 1976 presidential
candidate, who said Reagan had never properly atoned for
his 1967 blunder in signing California's liberalized abortion
law. McCormack herself ran for President again in 1980,
although her efforts were confined almost exclusively to
New York State. In speeches, she said Reagan's support of
a human life amendment was the result of a purely political
decision: "I think Reagan assessed the movement and . . . I
think he made the judgment that there is a powerful vote
potential there." She discounted Reagan's pledge to ap-
point antiabortion judges. He had promised an antiabortion
running mate, and had not delivered; why would the
promise about judges be any more meaningful?

As things turned out, McCormack was absolutely right.
In June 1981, Supreme Court Justice Potter Stewart announced his retirement. Reagan's choice to succeed Stewart
was Arizona Appeals Court Judge Sandra Day O'Connor,
whose voting record as an Arizona State senator had been,
for the most part, pro-choice. Paul Brown of LAPAC
called the O'Connor appointment a "betrayal," and NRLC
President Dr. Jack C. Willke wrote that Reagan had
"spurned the millions of sincere prolifers of both parties
who did vote for him—who did work for him—and who
just may not do it again." (Yet only three weeks earlier,
in writing, Reagan had reiterated his position that "inter-
rupting a pregnancy is the taking of a human life, and can
be justified only in self-defense—that is, if the mother's
own life is in danger.")

For a public official there is great risk in supporting a
human life amendment, as Reagan does. For if he truly believes that there is no moral difference between preventing

the implantation of a zygote and murdering a child, he is compelled to act with all possible speed, and by whatever means possible, to outlaw abortion. Reagan's appointment of a pro-choice judge—as well as his willingness to postpone action on the abortion question in favor of economic issues—showed that, at some level, he did perceive a difference.

When Reagan took office in January 1981, he and his aides made it clear that social issues on the conservative agenda, including abortion, would have to wait until the administration's economic program had cleared Congress. Hearings on a human life amendment were discouraged, and when freshman Senator John East—an ultraconservative protégé of Jesse Helms—held hearings on the Helms-Hyde bill defining human life as starting at the moment of fertilization, Reagan and his staff were reportedly distressed. They did not want attention drawn away from the President's plan to cut the budget and federal taxes.

Reagan's actions, or lack of them, show conclusively that he believes the act of abortion is not nearly as serious as the act of murder. While he was executing his tax cuts, legal abortions were taking place at the rate of better than four thousand a day. Were four thousand newborn babies being killed every day, Reagan would not have put the matter aside in favor of economics. Yet there is no reason to doubt the sincerity of his support of a human life amendment. But it is likely that his opposition to abortion has its roots, not in his attitude toward killing, but in his attitude toward sex.

We noted earlier that in 1969, as Governor of California, Reagan vetoed a bill which would have permitted the sale of prophylactics to minors—and that he did so for reasons of morality. The California Legislature had passed the bill in an effort to control an epidemic of venereal disease; Reagan's attitude was clearly that the proper way to avoid venereal disease was to behave in a chaste manner, and that people who engaged in what he considered excessive sexual activity should suffer the consequences. It is reasonable to believe that his opposition to abortion is based on the same philosophy. For if a human life amendment were truly a means of stopping murder, it would take precedence over budgets and tax cuts. But since it has nothing to do with murder, but is simply an instrument to punish sexually active women for their behavior, it can wait until the economy is healthy again.

CHAPTER 9

WOMEN AS *UNTERMENSCHEN*

Despite Reagan's failure to act quickly on the HLA, the right-to-life movement will probably endorse Ronald Reagan again in 1984, because from its point of view, a President who supports a human life amendment is preferable to one who opposes it—and if Reagan, from time to time, does things which indicate that he views abortion differently from murder, that is something the movement must live with.

But for the movement as a whole, it is an article of faith that abortion equals murder. According to them, the slaughter of fetuses that has occurred in the United States since the Supreme Court decision of 1973 is a continuing holocaust on a scale that dwarfs even the atrocities of Adolf Hitler and the Nazis during the last years of World War II. In fact, the holocaust metaphor is the heaviest piece of artillery in the movement's well-stocked propaganda arsenal.

The most articulate proponent of this theory is Dr. William Brennan, a mild, slightly built sociologist from Saint Louis University. In the summer of 1979, Brennan drew cheers from the delegates to the National Right to Life Convention in Cincinnati when he paralleled the extermination of Jews and other "undesirables" during the Third Reich with the deaths of millions of fetuses through abortions performed in the United States in the years following *Roe* v. *Wade* and *Doe* v. *Bolton.* Just as the Nazis declared Jews subhuman, he said, so the Supreme Court had declared the fetus less than human, and therefore expendable. His parallel extended to the technology that enabled the Nazis to quickly and efficiently kill millions of people, and the modern equipment that allows physicians to perform abortions quickly and cleanly.

He did not discuss the many fallacies of his analogy. He did not mention, for example, that the Third Reich was based on a philosophy that subjected individual civil rights to the whims of the state, while advances in the area of reproductive freedom in the United States came about during an era of expanding civil rights. He did not mention that under the Third Reich, laws concerning abortion were as severe and restrictive as those sought by his audience; Aryan women were required to produce new members of the Master Race, and were punished for having abortions, while women of "inferior" races were often forced to have abortions. In neither case did the concept of choice play a part. Similarly, Brennan failed to contrast Hitler's ideas regarding women with the feminist philosophy that was the driving force behind the movement for abortion on demand in America. In fact, Hitler's feelings about the proper role of women—*"Kinder, Kuche, Kirche"* (children, cooking, church)—much more closely paralleled those of most right-to-lifers than those of their opponents in the pro-choice movement.

Brennan stressed again and again the similarities he perceived in the roles played by *doctors* in the Third Reich and in the "holocaust" of fetuses in the United States. In each case, he said, it was the doctors who were most responsible for the killing, because they went along with what was legal, rather than objecting to it on moral grounds. He did not talk much about women.

A year later, Brennan had completed, and was awaiting the publication of, a two-volume work entitled *Medical Holocausts*, in which he expanded on his thesis of doctors as villains. During an interview at that time, he talked about how abortionists take advantage of women: "I think it's an exploitation of women that they're not aware of." He said women do not have a true picture of what goes on during an abortion. Women who seek abortions are not doing anything immoral, he said, it is the doctors, "because the doctors ought to know better. They're the ones who should have at least the biological facts about human development. And if they continue to promote abortion on demand, then I think they're held far more accountable than the women."

Brennan refuses to give women credit (or blame) for their own actions. He implies that women are unable to think independently, but are simply creatures manipulated by doctors and the media—passive vessels that things simply happen to. "We're all manipulated but not aware of it. We think we're being independent." If doctors would simply refuse to do abortions, he says, then there would *be* very few abortions, either legal or illegal.

This tendency to minimize the role of women in the matter of abortion is widespread in the antiabortion movement, and usually manifests itself in a manner that seems

benign. When right-to-lifers are asked who should be punished for abortions, they invariably answer that the physician in charge should be indicted (most say on a murder
charge), and that anyone who helped him (the physician is
always characterized as "him") should be indicted as an
accomplice. But what of the woman, the person who seeks
out and hires the "killer"? Dr. Jack C. Willke, president of
the National Right to Life Committee, answered:

> It's my firm position that I don't think any woman
> should ever be punished for having an abortion. Any
> more than we ever know of a cuckolded husband being
> punished for shooting his wife's lover in the bedroom
> when he walked in and found them there. There is
> simply a set of circumstances there that, in the over-
> whelming majority of women, will be operative. I could
> imagine some cold, ruthless prostitute type . . . but,
> y'know, that woman needs more pity than punishment
> in any case. On the other hand, the paid killer, the hit
> man, is not encumbered by those various emotional
> binds. That person would be calculating, cool, a paid
> executioner.

Willke understands that a woman is capable of thought,
that she is not mindless, "but I don't see her as involved,
in the sense that the person who took money for the deed,
who had no emotional involvement at all [is]. A woman
kills under emotional strain. Always."

Of course Willke is wrong about the cuckolds. Crimes
of passion are crimes, nevertheless, and are prosecuted as
such. His analysis of the bedroom murder, however, is consistent with his other thoughts on the subject of male-
female relations. A wife must never cheat on her husband,

but if she does, it is her lover—the man, the person in control—who is rightfully punished.

This concept of women as less than knowledgeable, capable human beings is widely accepted in the movement—and not just by men. Ann O'Donnell, a former vice president of the National Right to Life Committee, agrees that there should be no prosecution of women who seek out abortions. "Now maybe I'm taking . . . a chauvinistic attitude toward women, that they're poor little creatures, and they're just victims, and they really can't deal with it and they really don't understand what they're doing," she says. "I don't think a lot of them *do* understand what they're doing." O'Donnell speculates that women who seek abortions are both selfish and angry, and that they are taking out their hostility on the easiest victims: ". . . their anger is so great, their anger is so diverse, they're angry at the system, they're angry at men, they're angry at the baby, and the only person that they can really act out on is the baby. You know, the old thing about the lowest man on the totem pole."

But if women can be manipulated into having abortions, perhaps they can also be manipulated into having babies. Right-to-lifers do not call this manipulation, however. They call it pro-life counseling.

On the morning of Saturday, July 26, 1980, a young woman in a gray Mercedes sports car drove into the parking lot of the Del Crest Shopping Plaza in University City, Missouri, in Greater St. Louis. She parked, got out of the car, and walked toward the Ladies Center, a family planning clinic which provides abortion services on Saturday mornings. The woman appeared to be in her early twenties.

She was tall, and self-assured. She wore a green jersey and blue jeans.

Before she had taken a dozen steps, she was intercepted by a short, thin teenage girl. The girl showed the woman a pamphlet. The pamphlet was entitled "Life and Death," and the cover displayed a photo of a baby born alive at twenty-one weeks' gestation, and another photo of a reddish fetus labeled, "21 Week Baby Killed by Abortion." The teenager did not exactly block the woman's path, but walked extremely close to her; the woman veered slightly from side to side in order to avoid the girl. Their progress toward the clinic door was similar to that of two sailboats tacking into a wind.

The teenager was following standard procedure. According to a widely distributed right-to-life pamphlet entitled "Pro-Life Clinic Couselling: What Is It?" the most effecttive way to change a woman's mind about entering an abortion clinic is to:

Stand in front of her, talk to her gently, but continuously. Get her to respond to you, ask questions, get her to ask you questions, perhaps take her by the arm and lead her to the side. Get her away from the clinic door, if you can. It's too tempting. Keep talking, offer a cup of coffee at the cafe down the street.

Don't forget, you are really doing this for the mother. Approach it mainly from that standpoint. Remember she is going through hell. Realize this, gently let her know you understand, but in some subtle way let her know that there will be a far worse hell ahead, that she can never erase, if in fact she goes through with the abortion. Until the day she dies, she will never forget it. She can get rid of the baby in the womb . . . but never scrape it out of her mind.

Guilt, then, is the key to pro-life counseling, although not all counselors advocate such a direct approach. Sister Paula Vandegaer, editor of the antiabortion magazine *Heartbeat,* wrote in the Spring 1979 issue that it is tactically wrong to tell a pregnant teenager, "You'll murder your baby." Vandegaer added that there were "numerous ways to help her begin thinking about her baby," including the following lines:

> "I'm concerned about you, and I would like to tell you some things you might be interested in knowing about abortion."
>
> "I think you have some very difficult decisions to make and it is very important for you to know about each one of them: what to expect in keeping a baby; what to expect in placing a baby for adoption, and what to expect in aborting a baby."
>
> "You seem to feel that abortion is the answer. Have you thought of . . . "
>
> "I don't think they will tell you about this in the office where you go to have an abortion, but I want you to know . . ."

Thus, a subtle blend of guilt and compassion should do the trick. The underlying philosophy here appears to be that girls seeking abortions are not bad, but ignorant and desperate: "When a girl calls with a decision to abort we must talk to her long enough to slow her down," Sister Vandegaer writes.

Among some antiabortion "counselors" there is also another view—that any woman who even thinks about an abortion is simply not a good Christian. In El Cajon,

California, not far from Christian Heritage College, there is an organization called Family Life Seminars, which offers "Christian counseling" to troubled individuals and families. The director of Family Life Seminars is Dick LaHaye, brother of Tim LaHaye. Dick LaHaye says the problem of abortion does not occupy much of his time. If a woman is a good Christian, he says, "She'd have known in her own heart that . . . on the basis of Biblical teaching, it would have been wrong. Because we are to be fruitful and multiply. God didn't say for us to go out and kill our kids."

When right-to-lifers quote the Biblical injunction to be fruitful and multiply, they never finish the sentence. God told Adam and Eve, and later Noah, his sons, and their wives, "Be fruitful and multiply, *and replenish the Earth,*" which, at the time, was a reasonable thing for Him to say. In the case of Adam and Eve, the population of the Earth was a scant two; and when He gave the word to Noah and his sons, He had just drowned all but eight of the human beings on the planet. But the remaining eight eventually brought forth four billion progeny. It would seem that the job of replenishment has been handsomely accomplished.

Despite the right-to-lifers' frequent claims that the world is not, in fact, overpopulated, it seems far more likely that their primary interest in keeping women pregnant has to do with the status of the women themselves. Usually, when asked whether a woman has a right to control her own body, the antiabortionists answer yes, of course, but the fetus is not part of her body. In his book *Abortion, the Bible, and the Christian,* the Reverend Donald Shoemaker supplies a far more revealing answer: women do not, in fact, have the right to control their bodies, whether they are pregnant or not. Shoemaker cites two passages from Scripture to make his point:

> Or do you not know that your body is a temple of the Holy Spirit who is in you, whom you have from God, and that you are not your own? For you have been bought with a price, therefore glorify God in your body. (I Corinthians 6:19, 20)

and

> The wife does not have authority over her own body, but the husband does; and likewise also the husband does not have authority over his own body, but the wife does. (I Corinthians 7:4)

When it comes to determining the fate of her physical self, woman is third in line behind God and man. The fact that she has theoretical control over her husband's body must come as little comfort under such circumstances, since whether or not she is allowed to exercise this "control" is usually up to him.

It is not surprising that devotees of fundamentalist Protestant sects, along with adherents of other religions that relegate women to subservient roles—Catholicism, Mormonism, Orthodox Judaism, and Islam—oppose abortion. It is also not surprising that people who believe women should be subservient sometimes abandon the religion of their youth and embrace a faith more in keeping with their philosophy.

One such individual is a Virginia lawyer named Christian Streit White IV. In the spring of 1980, nearing his thirty-fifth birthday, he was still single. It was not that he hadn't tried, he said; it was simply that he had not yet found a woman who would say yes, and make it stick. Years earlier, it had been a woman who had driven him from the Episcopal Church.

He had been disenchanted with the church for a long time. He objected strongly to the clergy's attempts to appear trendy. A sermon preached on a theme presented in a Peanuts comic strip particularly offended him. He felt that if you were going to tell people that you were a faith of apostolic succession going back two thousand years, as the Episcopalians do, then it was your duty to maintain the faith, and not go scampering around preaching about comic strips. So he drifted away, without declaring a formal break. Then came the day when the leadership of his church made a lesbian a deaconness. An avowed, practicing lesbian.

To Christian White, the idea of a deaconess was bad enough. But a *lesbian*—a woman who behaved in a way that, to the best of his knowledge, every published version of the Bible described as abominable before the Lord—was more than he could tolerate. At that point, for him, the Episcopal Church ceased to be a church, and became instead a liberal social club. It was time to get out, and he did. He became a Malachite Greek Catholic. If you were going to have a religion, he thought, you might as well take it seriously.

He became involved with the issue of abortion while an undergraduate at the University of Virginia. At the time, he was also president of the local chapter of Young Americans for Freedom. He came by his politics naturally.

He belonged to an old Virginia family of German, English, Scotch, and Irish descent, with a pedigree sufficient for membership in good standing with the Daughters of the Confederacy and the Sons of the American Revolution. He had been told, although he had never checked, that one of his granduncles had been a governor of West Virginia, and another a Supreme Court judge of that state. His father had been president of the Waynesborough-East Augusta Democratic Club—the Byrd organization—from 1948 to 1962, and had never lost an election. "My daddy," Christian White was fond of saying, "taught me everything I know."

But his daddy had not taught him about abortion. That was left up to some local Catholics at the University of Virginia. One day they showed him what he now refers to as "the gory pictures." He "damn near puked," but the pictures got him involved.

By May 1980 White was research director for Judie Brown's American Life Lobby. In that capacity he attended the annual convention of one of their archenemies, the National Abortion Rights Action League, at the Hyatt Regency Hotel in Washington, D.C. Although the weather was hot and humid, he wore a midnight-blue three-piece pinstriped suit. He also wore a magnificent dark beard, spread out around his face in the style of southern aristocracy during the Civil War. His complexion was florid, his build ample. He told people that he was a lawyer with a private practice in Arlington, Virginia, which was true, as far as it went. His formal appearance set him apart from most of the other registrants, who tended to wear short-sleeved shirts or blouses, and slacks. But he appeared serene among the liberals. Even when he learned that his hosts knew who he was, he remained unruffled; he was left alone, and continued to attend various speeches and workshops. On the afternoon of May 30 he joined hundreds of pro-choice activists in the main meeting hall, and in this un-likely setting he consented to be interviewed.

"Once upon a time," he said, "I was a nubbin, so big . . ." He was holding his thumb approximately an eighth of an inch away from the end of his little finger. "Where the thumbnail lands is where the nubbin stops." He spoke slowly, drawing out certain words and phrases: "*nubbin,*" "*eighth* of an *inch.*" He paused, continued: "If that nub-bin had been killed, I would not be talking . . . today. It follows, then, that the nubbin was me. Since I am of the generic class, human being, it follows that the nubbin was a human being; therefore, by generalization, from one ob-servable object to all such identical objects, that *all* such nubbins are human beings. From which it follows that abortion is man-killing, and you don't do it lightly, if at all."

Any doctor who performs an abortion, White said, should be convicted of first-degree murder, as should nurses and anyone else who assists in the procedure—"willing, knowing accessories."

And what of the woman? She who wishes to rid herself of this burden? She who, by the millions, constitutes the *demand* side of the equation, without which the supply of doctors, nurses, clinics, drug manufacturers, and pro-choice politicians would fade away? What of her?

"For the woman involved, if she is a minor, or if it's her first, I would term it—and this is creating a new category of crime—aborticide," said Christian White. "And the first penalization would be a strictly corrective sentence

consisting of a year or eighteen months or whatever . . .
going into classes, teaching people not to do it again, *why*
not to. If it is a second time, or the first time for a woman
who had one as a minor, and went through the course and
the course didn't take, then, again, murder." Yet not first-
degree murder: "her closeness to the situation is likely to
skew her thinking a little bit, and therefore gives rise to a
reduced degree." Again there is the underlying assumption
that women seeking abortions—even those for whom the
abortion will not be the first—do not quite know what
they are doing; their thinking is skewed. When applied to
the more than one and a half million women who seek
abortions in the United States every year, and the approximately fifty million worldwide, it adds up to a sweeping
judgment on the capacity of women to think rationally
and make sound decisions.

Among right-to-lifers, this concept of women as creatures with diminished powers of reason is almost always
accompanied by a puritanical attitude about sex. Thus,
Christian White's thoughts on the revision of the criminal
code range far beyond abortion. They include, also, the
banning of all forms of artificial contraception. The manufacture of intrauterine devices and low-estrogen pills—the
suspected abortifacients—would become a serious felony.
Beyond that, mechanical contraceptives that prevent fertilization altogether—condoms, diaphragms, spermicidal
foams—would also be banned: ". . . on morality and also
social policy grounds, condoms, foams and such are used
with anybody at *any time.* They promote licentiousness.
Which is why they are most frequently sold in places such
as cheap bars. On the back of the men's room door."

It was pointed out that condoms are also sold on racks in drugstores.

"That, too," said White. "I have seen them in the drugstores on the 14th Street strip. [The 14th Street strip is Washington, D.C.'s red light district.] It is wall-to-wall dirty bookstores, dirty movie houses, burlesque shows; ladies of the evening congregate there in search of customers."

The problem with the sort of licentiousness promoted by artificial birth control, said White, is that "(a) it is a distinct threat to family structure; (b) it promotes a mindset of a shallow, short-sighted sort, which, if it is held by a sizable proportion of the population, renders the society less able to handle social problems."

White said that as a Malachite Greek Catholic he opposed even the so-called natural family planning, in which the condition of vaginal mucus is relied upon to indicate periods of fertility. But he added that natural family planning should be "permissible in terms of civil law." (This was comforting, since the only way to enforce a ban on natural family planning would be to monitor the whereabouts of every woman between the ages of twelve and fifty, every day, all the time.) Natural family planning methods, said White, were acceptable because they encourage moral behavior: "They require (a) self-discipline, and (b) fairly deep mutual knowledge. They therefore are most readily available in a state of marriage."

In fact, most people in the right-to-life movement share Christian White's distaste and fear of rampant sex; sex is something that must be kept under control at all costs. In February 1981, White's boss, American Life Lobby President Judie Brown, wrote in that organization's newsletter:

We know full well that our opposition, groups like
PLANNED PARENTHOOD, ZERO POPULATION GROWTH,
NATIONAL ORGANIZATION OF WOMEN [sic], and
many others, have told the public for years that the pill
and the IUD are just simply forms of "birth control."
We also know that the bottom line with these groups is
not as they would have us believe (i.e., assistance to
families who are faced with personal crises) but rather
their goal is a free-wheeling sexist society in which the
ego surmounts all else: removing the loving and cherish-
ing aspects of the marriage act and turning all human
beings into animals that cannot live without sex and related atrocities such as "easy abortion."

One of the current champions of the antiabortion movement, Senator Jeremiah Denton of Alabama, sees the
matter in remarkably simple terms: sexual permissiveness
is bad, and discipline is good. At a Senate hearing in the
spring of 1981 he lectured Planned Parenthood executives
Faye Wattleton and Barbara Maves:

> What I have seen of your stuff, I would think that you
> don't have enough emphasis on the essential idea of self-
> discipline, the importance of trying to be good. I am not
> standing here talking clothed in self-righteousness; I am
> not a man who has always been good, I am just a man
> who wants to be good, okay? And I believe my country
> better want to be good or it is not going to stay here
> much longer—free. Freedom is the luxury of self-disci-
> pline, and we are blowing it, blowing the whole concept.

And who shall be primarily responsible for seeing that this
discipline is carried out? According to Father Paul Marx, it
is up to women. In *The Death Peddlers*, Marx deplores

sexual freedom, equating it with promiscuity. He implies
that much of the blame for the deteriorating moral conditions he sees all around him is to be placed on the women's
liberation movement, and comes out strongly in favor of
the old sexual double standard:

> It is an almost inexplicable irony that the women's
> liberation movement, so valid in many respects, should
> espouse for women the truly degrading and destructive
> goals of easy abortion and sexual freedom (promiscuity).
> If in truth anatomy and biology can be so engineered as
> to alter woman's destiny, her innermost nature can be
> changed, if at all, only at tragic cost to herself and to
> the men who, rightly or wrongly, have always expected
> her to set society's moral standards. Far worse than the
> double standard of sexual morality, which made men
> unaccountable for their actions, is the single standard,
> which pushes women toward the same irresponsibility,
> with abortion as the equalizer.
>   The total tragedy was described by the far-seeing
> Benedictine Virgil Michel in 1936 when he observed,
> "The worst that can happen to a civilization is that its
> women descend to moral depths of unchristian men of
> the age."

Thus, Marx feels that the only proper place for a woman is
on her pedestal, and woe to her (and civilization) if she falls.

In their contempt for women who "descend to the
moral depths of unchristian men of the age"—as well as in
their contempt for homosexuals—right-to-lifers present an
attitude strikingly similar to that of the young Adolf Hitler.
Robert Payne, in *The Life and Death of Adolf Hitler*, relies
on testimony of an early friend of Hitler, August Kubizek:

Kubizek says [Hitler] never masturbated, detested sala-
cious jokes, and spoke about physical purity as though
he believed in some higher law that demanded purity
in men and women. A hermit by deliberate choice,
Adolf despised homosexuals as much as he despised the
women he sometimes encountered at the opera who
indicated that they would welcome his advances.

Abortion, of course, allows women to come down from
the pedestal without paying the traditional penalty of enforced motherhood. All of which raises the question: Are
right-to-lifers more concerned with the fate of the fetus, or
with the "unrestrained sexuality" they see coming about
as a result of abortion on demand? A study conducted by
the Quixote Center, an institute of progressive Catholics,
points toward the latter conclusion. "If 'pro-life' is an ac-
curate description of the anti-abortion movement, then
views favorable to a 'Human Life Amendment' should cor-
relate positively and strongly with other 'pro-life' stands:
opposition to the death penalty, a concern for racial equal-
ity (because inequality has led to violence against Black
people), and something less than total reliance on the U.S.
military for security." Yet when the Center polled 2,718
Catholics who favored the human life amendment, it
found "a moderate negative association" with this pro-life
index. In a subsequent set of questions, those favoring the
human life amendment were asked about their views on
sex and marriage, as well as birth control, remarriage after
divorce, and priestly celibacy. The study—which was published in 1978 under the title "Are Catholics Ready?"—
showed that "views on an anti-abortion amendment were

much more strongly associated with views about sex and
marriage than with opinions on 'pro-life' issues . . . those
favoring such an amendment were much more likely than
opponents to lean toward traditional positions on marriage
and sexuality issues." The study concluded:

> These findings call into serious question the claim of the
> anti-abortion movement to the title "pro-life." They in-
> dicate that the movement derives its most fundamental
> motivations less from a reverence for human life than
> from a concern for sexual morality.

If this is true, then it follows that all of the right-to-lifers'
talk of murder and holocaust is simply a device to keep
their opponents on the defensive, and a screen for the true
concern of the movement—the preservation of repressive
puritanical sexual mores.

CHAPTER 10

SCENES FROM A CONVENTION

In the summer of 1980, at the Eighth Annual National Right to Life Convention in Anaheim, California, evidence of this puritanical attitude was not hard to find. There, at the Convention Center, in a large room set aside for the display of antiabortion goods and services, a handsome, grandmotherly woman named Mrs. Patricia B. Driscoll stood behind the counter of a booth devoted entirely to chastity. The name of the organization Mrs. Driscoll represented was Christian Womanity. Among the posters for sale at the booth were the following:

Sexual Abstinence = Sexual Freedom

Great for Guys, Too! Abstinence Makes
the Heart Grow Fonder

Abstinence Works

Be Special—Be a Virgin

Everybody Isn't Doing It—
Be Smart Too—Save Sex for Marriage

Be Square With Flair—Stay Virgin

Now It's In—Secondary Virginity

Mrs. Driscoll explained that a secondary virgin is someone who has been sexually active in the past but has seen the error of his or her ways. Asked how her organization felt about contraceptives, she said, "We are for the integrity of the sex act—before *and* after marriage." If one *must* limit the size of one's family, she said, one should use natural family planning. Mrs. Driscoll said proudly that she had "four sons, seven daughters, three grandchildren, and one husband."

The Anaheim Convention Center is a concrete igloo set amidst a flat sprawl of motels and fast-food operations a mile from Disneyland. The convention did not begin until Thursday, June 25, but delegates representing National Right to Life Committee affiliates across the country had been arriving since Wednesday evening. They stood in groups in the lobbies of their hotels, getting reacquainted. Many wore Reagan-for-President buttons.

But the National Right to Life Committee was not the only antiabortion group in Anaheim that week. Paul Brown of the Life Amendment Political Action Committee had rented a suite of rooms in a hotel called the Inn at the Park, which is separated from the Convention Center by only a parking lot. Brown and LAPAC were running their own workshops, holding their own press conferences, openly defying the NRLC's claim to pre-eminence. Some right-to-lifers with contacts in both camps scurried back and forth across the parking lot, smiling grimly, reminding themselves, perhaps, that there were babies to be saved.

On Thursday evening, in a large auditorium in the Convention Center, a group of clean, white boys wearing white turtlenecks, red blazers with American flag patches on the sleeves, navy blue slacks, and spit-shined black shoes formed three rows on a stage. Under the direction of their leader, Father Richard Coughlin, the boys sang "If My Friends Could See Me Now" as NRLC delegates drifted into the room. A fair number of the delegates carried babies.

Each baby that shows up at a right-to-life gathering is a statement. However, when any of the babies cry, nobody ever remarks that this or that baby seems unhappy, or, perhaps, that a baby's screaming is drowning out the words of an important speaker. It is bad form to talk of babies that way. It is the firm conviction of many right-to-lifers that anyone who favors legal abortion hates babies. It is important, therefore, to carry babies around, and to indulge them at all times.

The chorus took a break. A singer climbed onstage. He was a handsome man of medium build, with slick dark hair, country-and-western style. He was Sean Morton Downey, Jr., formerly a lobbyist for the NRLC, now a board member of LAPAC. His father was a famous Irish tenor, but his own voice was unexceptional. He sang two songs. The first was "Danny Boy." The second was called "Got a Right to Live." It was his own composition, sung from the point of view of a fetus. At the close of this number he received a generous round of applause.

He left the auditorium quickly, however. He had many differences of opinion with the NRLC, his former employer.

One of these concerned the man who would be the featured speaker on the night's program, Dr. Bernard Nathanson, the former master abortionist who had now converted to the antiabortion cause. Sean Morton Downey thought the inclusion of Nathanson in the program was a disgrace. As far as Downey was concerned, Nathanson's motives were mercenary. He made money from abortions, Downey thought, and now, with his book, *Aborting America,* he was trying to make money from the antiabortion movement. Downey had read Nathanson's book, and found too much bravado and no remorse. "I respect Bill Baird more than I respect Nathanson," Downey would say later. Within the right-to-life movement the name of abortion rights activist Baird is a curse, but to Downey, at least, Baird stood up for what he believed in, in his own way, without making a lot of money. Nathanson, Downey thought, was trying to con people. And so Downey departed. He would not shake Nathanson's hand, would not be in the room when he spoke.

Timothy Cardinal Manning of Los Angeles offered the invocation. Lean and concave, Manning had a sepulchral voice that rose near the end of each phrase:

"Merciful Father . . . forgive those who suffocate and slaughter life at its uterine beginnings . . . forgive them, for they know not what they *do;* surgeons and their co-operators who do this for money are selling life for *Ju*das *pie*ces of *si*lver . . . Let them see the enormity of their crime, and the consequences of its unrepenting. Enlighten the minds of the lawmakers that they may undo the havoc that brings our nation to the edge of decom*po*sing . . ."

When Manning finished, the chairman of the convention, the Reverend Donald P. Shoemaker, author of *Abortion, the Bible, and the Christian*, stepped forward. He wore a neat black beard and a leisure suit. His opening remarks reflected the determination of the National Right to Life Committee Board of Directors to be bipartisan and ecumenical, to reach across the whole political and religious spectrum for support. (This was one of the reasons the NRLC considered Dr. Bernard Nathanson such a catch; he was an atheist of Jewish origin.) Shoemaker said, "Either we are to be white and conservative, or we can broaden our base and have a human life amendment." He singled out a woman who belonged to a splinter group called Feminists for Life. Elizabeth Moore, thirty-seven, had never been married, although she had six children. Unlike the vast majority of delegates, Moore favored the Equal Rights Amendment and opposed Ronald Reagan. But of course she favored a human life amendment. Shoemaker said, "I love it because she's so untypical."

Two other speakers also tried to capture this spirit of political ecumenicalism. Dr. Jack C. Willke, the president-elect of the NRLC who would take over that office the following day, remarked that the only thing many pro-lifers had in common was, in fact, their opposition to abortion. He cited with approval California State Senator David Roberti, who sponsored gay rights legislation but also favored a human life amendment. (Paul Brown and Father Paul Marx of LAPAC would later severely criticize Willke for this remark.)

California State Senator John G. Schmitz then made a weak attempt to put any liberals in the audience at ease with a joke. Schmitz, a fervent right-winger, said "For those of you who are liberal, and think that Orange County is a place full of right-wingers, rest assured—the state delegation from Orange County is not even here now. They're down in Chile studying campaign techniques." This jocular reference to the brutally repressive regime of Augusto Pinochet drew a roar of laughter.

Dr. Willke read a letter which presidental candidate Ronald Reagan had sent to the convention. It said:

> Never before has the cause you espouse been more important to the future of our country. The critical values of the family and the sanctity of human life that you advocate are being increasingly accepted by our citizens as essential to reestablishing the moral strength of our nation.

Dr. Willke relinquished the microphone to Dr. Carolyn Gerster, who introduced Dr. Bernard Nathanson. Nathanson wore a gray suit and black-rimmed glasses. He spoke diffidently, yet with gusto, about his days as a master abortionist. "We did one hundred and twenty abortions a day," he said. "A five-million-dollar-a-year business . . . a *five-million-dollar-a-year* business! Think, think now, how many handicapped children could have been helped, how much cancer research could be done, how many operations of a decent sort could have been carried out on poor people, for that kind of money." The delegates cheered, although Nathanson offered no evidence that cancer research, or operations of "a decent sort," declined when abortion became legal.

Nathanson briefly outlined the evolution of thought

that brought him from a proabortion position to the right-to-life viewpoint. "I have been reviled, attacked, assaulted, insulted, degraded by those who say that a change of opinion is hypocritical, and wrong, but in the words of William Blake, 'The man who never changes his opinions is like stagnant water, and breeds reptiles in the mind,'" he said with defiant pride. "I do not want my mind to be an aquarium for reptiles."

Nathanson received a prolonged ovation from the two thousand delegates in the room. Then the lights dimmed and a large movie screen was lowered.

It is, of course, an article of faith among right-to-lifers that there is no moral difference between abortion and murder. Upon this article of faith the movement has built a series of assumptions about people who favor abortions, and people who don't. Some of these assumptions were presented to the delegates in the premiere of a film called *Assignment: Life.* In the film, an actress portraying a fictional newspaper reporter named Anne Summers sets out to get "both sides of the story" on the abortion issue.

Scene: Anne interviews Dr. Edward Allred, who operates thirteen abortion clinics in California. Allred says, "I really believe that this is essential as a matter of population control, as a matter of suppressing poverty, crime, and all other kinds of human problems in our society." The audience hissed. (Underlying assumption: Abortionists see the killing of babies, i.e., fetuses, as one way to solve society's problems.)

Scene: Anne interviews a woman who is a marriage and family counselor.

ANNE: "Do you look upon abortion as a birth control method?"

COUNSELOR: "I do not look upon abortion as a birth control method at all. I do not support using it as a birth control method. But when it comes down to having an unwanted child, I would support abortion."

ANNE: "Have you had an abortion?"

COUNSELOR: "Yes, I have had several." (Gasps from the audience.) "I do not know what it would have been like if I had not been able to make that choice, to have an abortion. I would have had three children now and probably have been on welfare."

ANNE: "Are you married?"

COUNSELOR: "No, I'm not."

ANNE: "What about adoption?"

COUNSELOR: "That, to me, personally, would be so enormously painful I could not ever have that as a choice. So I don't feel it *is* a choice for many women." (Assumptions: Unmarried women who are sexually active use abortion as a back-up birth control method. They are so selfish that they would rather murder their own children than go through with the pregnancies and give the babies up for adoption.)

Scene: The director of administration for five California birth control clinics tells Anne that one third of the abortion patients are minors: "Probably ninety percent of these would not have told their parents." (Assumption: Laws that allow teenagers to have abortions without parental consent are undermining the family.)

Scene: At Casa Theresa, a "Christian-based" home for unwed mothers, Anne asks a pregnant girl named Cathy,

"What's helped you the most in getting through the past nine months?"

As music wells up in the background, Cathy says, "I honestly feel that it was God. If there wasn't a God out there I would have never made it. My life was just torn, practically, and He's really pieced it back together." (Assumption: Any woman who truly opens herself to God will come to see that abortion is a sin.)

Scene: Anne interviews a former topless dancer who has seen the error of her ways. (The right-to-life movement contains a significant number of ex-sybarites who have gone from one extreme to the other. Another of these, ex-Playboy bunny Brenda Miller, would appear at the convention the following day.) The woman says, "We're living in a society that is very pleasure-oriented. Do whatever feels good and worry about the consequences later. I believe in discipline. Nobody has to get pregnant today if they don't want to. And very seldom is it a husband and wife and they goofed and they got pregnant. Most of it is in the back seat of a van by teenagers that are unwed in a fit of passion. We're not teaching our children to abstain. I'm a Christian and I believe that sex is something sacred. It's not something that is spread all over town. (More music in the background.) I feel that abortion, gonorrhea, syphilis are getting out of kilter. And I think that God created the family, I believe that babies are supposed to have both mother and father, and I believe that if we had done it the way God planned it, we wouldn't be in the situation we're in now." (Assumption: Sex for pleasure is sinful. Abstinence is the only acceptable conduct for the unmarried.)

Scene: A backyard. A happy little adopted boy plays

with his parents. The mother says, "He could have been one of those abortion statistics. So I would say, Please don't. Go ahead and have the child and give someone else a chance to make him their own." (Assumption: Women who have abortions are selfishly murdering children who could make other people happy.)

Scene: Anne attends the 1980 March for Life in Washington, D.C. There she encounters Dr. and Mrs. Jack C. Willke, and asks for an interview. Dr. Willke says, "Gee, we're busy right now with the march . . ."

They meet at the Willkes' hotel. Willke produces the visual aids he uses at every public performance. He displays photographs of fetuses at twenty-one weeks, sixteen weeks, fourteen weeks ("You'll notice he's sucking his thumb"), eight weeks, six weeks. He plays a tape recording of the heartbeat of a fetus at eight weeks. It sounds like a locomotive going through a tunnel.

Then he shows his gory pictures. "This is what's left after a typical safe, legal suction abortion. Here we have about a two-and-a-half month baby [he means fetus] . . . that suction has just torn the body of that baby to pieces." Willke did not show pictures of the results of typical *illegal, unsafe* abortions, perhaps because the bloody, dying mother would draw attention away from the fetus.

When the movie ended and the lights went on, a young man named Bill Smith was introduced. He had long brown hair and a receding hairline. He wore a flowered shirt and carried a large backpack. In 1979 he had gained brief national attention by walking from his home in San Diego to Washington, D.C., to dramatize his opposition to abortion.

The film has shaken Smith. "I've never seen those pictures before," he says. "We'll have to go after those clinics. They're no different than Auschwitz." He walked off the stage, knelt down facing a wall, and wept.

The next morning in an interview, Dr. Jack Willke, the president of the National Right to Life Committee, and Dr. Carolyn Gerster, the ex-president, tried to explain to me why the National Right to Life Committee, as opposed to Paul Brown's LAPAC, represented the mainstream of right-to-life thought. Gerster noted that while LAPAC consisted solely of a five-person board of directors, the NRLC "has eleven to thirteen million members."

"That's a big range," I said.

"That's because we don't have a body count," Gerster said. "We have to estimate state organizations. These are not people working in the offices—but these are people who will march with us, vote with us, who will attend conventions, that kind of thing."

"See, we don't count by dues-paying members," Dr. Willke said.

"How many dues-paying members are there?" he was asked.

"It's not a measure in any way," he said. "Let me give you an example. In our own city of Cincinnati, we have an independent Baptist church that has twenty-four thousand people at Sunday services. This [preacher] is so pro-life that he's cut records on it, he preaches on it. He's the Jerry Falwell type on this issue. Not a one of those people that we know of belongs to our organization. None of them pay dues."

"But you are counting them among . . ."

"Every one of those is with us when the ballot boxes are counted, you see. Now, we distribute eighty thousand newsletters in a city of a million—we do that monthly. This congregation doesn't get any of them. The preacher gets half a dozen. He takes things out of it and puts it in his bulletin. But here's twenty-four thousand—when you take the children off—what, seven thousand homes, you see. Fourteen thousand voters, or more. Yet they wouldn't in any way appear . . . they don't come to our meetings, even . . ."

"So, your estimate of eleven to thirteen million is not terribly scientific."

"Oh, no," said Dr. Jack C. Willke. "But it wins elections."

The interview was cut short as the hierarchy of the National Right to Life Committee interrupted us and prepared to hold a press conference. They taped to the walls color photographs of fetuses in various stages of development: six weeks, eight weeks, eleven, fourteen, eighteen weeks. They also taped up a photograph of tiny human feet, the feet of a fetus at ten weeks. About twenty reporters entered the room. Dr. Willke said, "Basically we are a civil rights organization. The fact of human life in the womb is a simple scientific fact. Alive, yes. And growing from the time of fertilization. That's biologic simplicity."

He added, "We are not lacking in compassion for the woman who carries the child. Our members, our officers, *far* beyond the national average, are caring, concerned people. We are deeply concerned about the mother, but we

have never felt—and we feel very strongly about this—that
our nation should give to one individual the complete legal
right to kill another in order to solve that first individual's
personal, social, or health problems."

Dr. Willke introduced Dr. Bernard Nathanson. Nathanson assailed the pro-choice movement for using a coat-
hanger as a symbol of the kind of desperate measures
women would resort to if abortion is outlawed. The coat-
hanger is outmoded, said Nathanson. There is a family of
drugs called prostaglandins which induce abortions. Were
abortion outlawed, it would be "a very simple matter to
go to the drugstore, or to a physician, and obtain a prescription for prostaglandins." The drugs themselves would
not be outlawed, he said, since they have many uses outside of abortion. "There will be no more back-alley butch-
ers, women mutilated, broken, or permanently crippled,"
he said. "That is the stereotype provoked or pushed by the
proabortion—abortophile—movement against this organization and what it stands for. But it is deceitful, it is wrong,
and it is, above all, irrelevant, and now, historically, an
anachronism."

He seemed to be saying that even if abortions were
outlawed women would have no problem obtaining them.
He did not mention that prostaglandins are extremely
powerful drugs which can produce harmful side effects,
nor did he mention that, were abortions to be outlawed,
doctors and pharmacists would undoubtedly be subject to
prosecution for prescribing prostaglandins for abortions.
Doctors and pharmacists inclined to break the law in this
manner would expect considerable remuneration. Thus,
the situation would revert to the way it was before 1973:

wealthy women would be able to obtain abortions, while poor women would again be left to their own devices, including coathangers.

Brenda Miller, the former Playboy bunny, now assistant producer of the Christian Broadcasting Network's "700 Club," was the next speaker. She had a round face, large dark eyes, and shiny black hair cut short, with bangs down to her eyebrows. She spoke in a high, childlike voice, as though reciting. During her bunny days, she said, abortion was a way of life. But then she came to know the Lord and have a respect for life. "The Scripture says that our God knit us together in our mothers' wombs, and there I knew that the reality of life began. As well as the scientific fact, there was the religious fact. So I feel called to speak out to let my friends know, to let the people who may be living that life, who may be thinking that abortion is right, abortion is good, it is the only way, that it is *not* the way, and that you are surely committing murder by taking the life of that child." She said it was only through "the grace of God" that she, herself, did not have to have an abortion during those hedonistic days.

Miller was followed by Erma Clardy Craven, a formidable black woman who was anything but childlike. Craven a sixty-two-year-old social worker from Minnesota, said, "I view the pro-choice movement in this country as elitist, racist, and genocidal. I unequivocally compare it with what happened in Hitler's Germany." She added, "I would like to remind white America that black women gave birth to white children at very tender ages. Thirteen, fourteen, fifteen years of age. You have seen *Roots* and you have seen *Holocaust*. And you know what the black woman has contributed to America." Craven announced that her participation in the right-to-life movement was "in the interest of black womanhood." She did not explain the connection between black women's contributions to America and the need to force black women to bear children they did not want.

During a question-and-answer period, Dr. Carolyn Gerster was asked why the NRLC was against abortion even in cases of rape. Gerster said that pregnancy from rape "occurs very, very seldom as compared to consenting intercourse. [But] it certainly occurs. If the treatment for rape is given within forty-eight hours, pregnancy is virtually zero." This was a truly remarkable statement, for it contradicted the National Right to Life Committee's official position that from the time of fertilization, a zygote should be protected. The most frequent treatment given rape victims to prevent pregnancy is the drug diethylstilbestrol (DES), which operates as a "morning-after-pill"— that is, it prevents the implantation of the already fertilized egg in the uterus. Technically, it is an abortifacient. Gerster's contention appeared to imply that zygotes resulting from rape do not become persons quite as quickly as do zygotes resulting from consenting intercourse.

As the press conference wound down, Dr. Willke said, "Thought you might be interested in hearing the heartbeat of an unborn child at the time when a mother is just missing her second menstrual period." He held up a tape recorder; again there was a sound like a locomotive moving through a tunnel.

A few minutes after the NRLC press conference ended, Paul Brown, the director of LAPAC, and Robert Sassone, LAPAC's legal adviser, called a press conference of their own in the Inn at the Park. They announced that LAPAC had filed suit against every Catholic diocese in the fifty states. Brown explained that the purpose of the suit was not to harass the bishops, but to free them from an Internal Revenue Service regulation preventing single-issue groups from distributing political literature on church property. The church, he said, had been reluctantly going along with this ruling for fear of losing its tax-exempt status. But he also said, "The effect of the bishops' position in prohibiting distribution of material on church property is to protect church net income at the expense of the innocent blood of millions of pre-born babies."

Back at the Convention Center, a singer named Jeff Steinberg entertained the NRLC delegates during lunch. Steinberg is about three feet tall. He was born without arms. Both legs were deformed. Extensive surgery provided him with a foreshortened right arm with a hook at the end, and he is able to walk. His repertoire, he said, was made up of "Christian music." As a pianist played background music, Steinberg delivered a between-songs patter: ". . . but y'know folks, what if Jeff Steinberg had not been allowed to live? What if . . . what if somebody had thought they were smart enough . . . to decide what I should or shouldn't be? How many lives . . . could be challenged and touched . . . and motivated . . . by somebody who's not existent . . . because a doctor did something he wasn't supposed to do . . . or because *some*body made a decision . . . in haste? . . ."

He sang a song called "Statue of Liberty":

The Cross . . .
Is my Statue of Liberty . . .
It was there
That my soul was made free . . .

Then he introduced his wife, who is not handicapped. And he plugged his album, which was on sale in back of the room.

Steinberg received a standing ovation. To the right-to-lifers he was living proof of the evil represented by the March of Dimes, Planned Parenthood, and others who would make it easy for a pregnant woman to abort a genetically defective fetus. The movement strongly opposes the procedure called amniocentesis, which is used to detect Down's Syndrome and other genetic defects in fetuses. The right-to-lifers say that every baby should be given a chance to live, no matter how horribly deformed or mentally defective it might be. To destroy these fetuses, they say, is to set up an elitist society in which only the perfect may live. It is the first step toward the breeding of a master race, the Third Reich reincarnate.

Less than a month earlier, the movement had scored a great victory when the Southern Baptist Convention had reversed a nine-year stand in favor of choice and come out against abortion. This had been accomplished under the leadership of the conference's new president, the Reverend Dr. Bailey Smith, who was on record as saying that "God does not hear the prayers of a Jew" and that "Jews have funny noses."[1] He later apologized for both remarks.

A promotional brochure about Jeff Steinberg said that he was born Jewish, but that his conversion to Christianity had made him a "completed Jew."

Friday afternoon, at a LAPAC workshop at the Inn at the Park, Murray Norris, the distributor of the booklet "Who Killed Junior?," talked about the power of God. The answer to the evils of abortion, pornography, homosexuality, and the evils of secular humanism lay in the power of prayer, he said. It was that simple. Take the case of the guy in Portland, Oregon, he said, who was going to give a rock 'n' roll concert during which he would call up the spirit of Elvis. A clear case of satanism.

"What happened?" somebody asked.

"The people really turned out," said Norris. "But the Christians, a lot of them, carried their picket signs up and down in front of this concert. Y'know, objecting to satanism or witchcraft or whatever . . . the smart ones, they rented a room right next door. And they spent their time in prayer, binding the spirits. The concert was such a case of confusion they never got around to the séance."

The same power of prayer that prevented the séance should be used in politics, said Norris. "Because the Bible says when the righteous are in power, the people are happy. But look at it. Who do they mean by 'righteous'? They mean the people who are Christian, the people who believe in God. I mean I'm not trying to exclude any others . . . like the Jews, for example, but what I'm saying is, people who understand what God wants. These are the righteous ones, and these are the ones He's expecting to rule."

After a full day of conference activities, Friday evening brought two arrivals from the east coast. One was Dr. Mildred Faye Jefferson, former NRLC president, now director of her own organization, the Right-to-Life Crusade, and LAPAC board member. She had not yet been told that her fellow board members, Brown and Sassone, had filed suit against the Catholic Church.

The other traveler was a man, white, in his late forties, a loner by all accounts. He was lean and fit, with shiny black hair and a round face, which was by turns angelic, mischievous, bratty. He hated everything the right-to-life movement stood for. He was in Anaheim because the enemy was in Anaheim. The right-to-lifers knew he was there; his presence became part of their state of mind. To them it was as though Hitler himself were prowling the corridors. "Did you see him?" "Who?" "Bill Baird." *"Here?"*

Mildred Jefferson addressed about two hundred people at the LAPAC gathering. Her speech was a masterpiece, playing powerfully upon the fear in her audience, the terror of change. The family. The humanists want to change the very foundation of society, the family! She said:

"What difference should it make to us that a collection of many sorts of people come together and say, 'Oh, well, we are a family too'? It may not matter at all—if there were not the attempt to force the model on the rest of society." And:

"Nothing can be left alone. The whole thing is to destroy the structure, the form, the custom, and the foundation of law that is represented in the traditional posture of our country. The traditional social forms are the things that must be destroyed."

She was unable to ignore the presence of Baird. She referred to him only as "my little friend." She was in control. She said, "I don't have anger, he cannot provoke me to rage." She said that while it was not her place to judge, she knew there would be a day of reckoning, "and when he has to stand judged by Him from whom we all came, what kind of defense can he give? So I don't have to be angry with him. I can smile at him. I can look at him cloaked in the sense of Christian charity."

The next morning, Saturday, the devil was still at hand. But so, too, was the reigning saint of the right-to-life movement, Congressman Henry J. Hyde. The saint and the devil encountered one another briefly as Hyde entered the auditorium of the Convention Center. Baird challenged Hyde to a debate. Hyde replied loftily that there were only three people in the world with whom he would refuse to share a platform: "Charles Manson, Richard Speck, and Bill Baird." Inside the auditorium, Dr. Jack C. Willke recounted this episode during his introduction of Hyde. The NRLC delegates applauded wildly.

Hyde spoke at length about the elitists and the intellectuals his audience loved to hate. His message was simple: We are the good guys, they are the bad guys. In closing, he said, "I've talked about institutional selfishness, the 'Me Generation.' But these appellations do not describe the pro-life movement. *Our* pro-life movement. Selfless rather than selfish. Its rewards are in caring and loving other

members of the human family we will never see and
never know."

It is apparently much easier for right-to-lifers to care
for and love such remote and abstract members of the
human family than it is for them to love members of their
own. This, at least, was the contention of a booklet on sale
at the booth of the Right to Life Society of Greater Cleve-
land. The booklet was entitled "Why Do Pro-Lifers Hate
Each Other So Much? (And What Can Be Done About It?)."
The booklet opens with four brief, discordant scenes, including the following:

"That incompetent ass!"

Sally was upset. Bob was late again in publishing the
local pro-life newsletter. What good did it do to an-
nounce important events after they had happened?

"He's got to go," she vowed. Two months later she had
her way when Bob was purged from the local organization.

And:

"Pro-life—pro-life—pro-life . . . That's all I ever hear,"
complained Jack. "Every night you're gone with those
fanatics. When is it going to stop?"

"Why don't you come with me?" Alice asked her husband for the two-hundredth time.

"I wouldn't be caught dead with that narrow little
clique," Jack replied. "They spend more time fighting
each other than they do saving babies."

212 Enemies of Choice

The author of the booklet, Joseph P. Meissner, attributes
the friction within the movement to antiabortionists' frustration over the inability to act:

> ... we pro-lifers cannot resort to ... acts of violence
> no matter how we are provoked, no matter how much
> we may be justified. So what happens? Our frustrations
> increase. We lose sight of our goal. We lash out at those
> around us.

Pro-life activity may even threaten marriages. "How many
of the following sentiments have you heard?" he asks his
readers:

> "Honey, do you have to go to that pro-life meeting
> tonight?"
>
> "I'm tired of taking our vacations so we can go to a pro-
> life convention."
>
> "I have to do all my pro-life work during the day when
> my husband's at work. That way he doesn't know and
> get upset ..."
>
> "My wife just doesn't understand why I'm involved. She
> keeps asking what I get out of this."
>
> "If you go to one more meeting, then maybe you'd bet-
> ter stay away."
>
> "I wonder what it would be like to be married to a
> spouse who was as involved as I am ..."

Following Henry Hyde's speech, it became apparent that
things were not going well within the "family" of official
antiabortion organizations. Dr. Jack C. Willke made a

dramatic announcement to the NRLC delegates; he read LAPAC's press release detailing the lawsuit to be filed against the Catholic dioceses. The press release was headlined,

30 PIECES OF SILVER LAWSUIT FILED
AGAINST U.S. CATHOLIC BISHOPS

Suddenly, the devil was no longer the fellow in the corridor; the devil was within. Another NRLC official, the Reverend John Waddey, read a statement dissociating the NRLC from LAPAC:

> The National Right to Life Committee, its Board of Directors, and its thirteen million members from every state in America, wish to publicly dissociate ourselves from this attempt to slur those who share our pro-life commitment. Furthermore, we wish to compliment those Catholics who not only work to save lives, but are suffering from a resurgence of anti-Catholic bigotry.

(Members of the right-to-life movement have long attempted to associate the pro-choice movement with anti-Catholic bigotry. It was no wonder, then, that the NRLC hierarchy was upset when an organization on its own side of the abortion issue attacked the church.)

As Waddey walked away from the microphone, Dr. Mildred Faye Jefferson climbed, uninvited, to the stage. Although purged by the leadership two years earlier, Dr. Jefferson was still popular among the NRLC delegates. She approached the microphone, paused for effect, and said with feeling, "For those of you who don't know me, my name is *Mildred Faye Jefferson.*" She paused again, then said, "I am the vice president of the board of directors [of LAPAC] and I was not consulted about this action. I found out about it yesterday and I thought some-one was making a joke until someone actually gave me a copy of the press release.

"We had a board meeting last night and I indicated that within a family you do not bring suit against family members. (Applause.) I've indicated that if the action were not rescinded at the earliest possible moment...that it would be necessary for me to withdraw all support from LAPAC." (Sustained applause.)

Just before the session broke up, Dr. Carolyn Gerster took the microphone. Dr. Gerster has five sons. She also had two miscarriages, and gave birth to a sixth boy who died in infancy. The *New York Times Magazine* of March 30, 1980, quoted her as saying that she had wanted a girl, and when the boy died, "I got crazy. I thought I had wished that kid away..." Dr. Gerster warned the delegates that pro-choice demonstrators were expected to picket the Convention Center in the afternoon. "They are trying to label us antifeminist," she said. "The *real* victim of the proabortion mentality in the women's movement *is* the women's movement. The anger that should have been di-rected against the male oppressor has been diverted to the unborn child of the woman's womb. And, friends, you cannot enhance a woman's rights by denying the most basic right of all to her unborn daughter."

Meanwhile, at Stoddard Park, about a mile east of the Convention Center, the pro-choice demonstrators gathered under the banner of ARC (Abortion Rights Coalition). They were predominantly young, dressed in blue jeans and T-shirts; most sat on the grass, enjoying the sun. The atmosphere was similar to that of the milder antiwar demonstrations of the sixties. A series of booths was set up. At the Atheist Information Booth there was a portrait of Pope John Paul II, with a fiendish grin, strangling a woman; "Public Enemy Number One," it said. There were other signs and posters, among them:

Wanted Kids Have Better Parents

Keep Your Laws Off My Body

Sexism Is a Communicable Disease

Don't Force Me to Follow Your Religion—
Separate Church and State

No More

A small airplane circled the park towing a banner:

Keep Abortion Legal—Bill Baird Center—Boston

A number of women gave speeches. Then the demonstrators marched to the Convention Center, where they picketed peacefully and put on pro-choice skits.

Meanwhile, inside the Convention Center, a press release on LAPAC stationery was circulated. It carried a statement from Sean Morton Downey, who had been

installed as LAPAC president the day before. Downey said
the suit against the Catholic Church would be withdrawn—
that it had served its purpose.

Back in the auditorium, Congressman Robert Dornan
made a speech. Dornan is the House sponsor of the no-
exceptions human life amendment. He told a story about
his father, Harry Dornan, who died at the age of eighty-
three. Two weeks before he died, Harry told Robert,
"'Y'know, son, it probably is no tragedy for me to get out
of this world, my bags are packed. I've lived several lives
and it's all been a snap of the fingers.'" Congressman
Robert Dornan said the mission of the right-to-lifers was of
"massive, galactic proportions." He said, "We just know
that some day, some day at the snap of the fingers, passing
to our eternity, we're going to meet millions of human beings, aborted souls, who will say, 'You either saved my life,
or you tried.'"

On Sunday morning, the last day of the convention,
two young men sat and talked in a hotel coffee shop. One
was Bill Smith, who walked from San Diego to Washington
in 1979 and who broke down in tears on stage following
the movie Friday night. The other was Samuel Lee of St.
Louis. Lee is tall, thin, angular. His face has two prominent
features: an enormous, ragged beard and his metal-framed
glasses. Lee is a veteran organizer of sit-ins at abortion
clinics in St. Louis. Bill Smith said the two were disap-
pointed with the convention. "Some of us in the San Diego
area have decided it's time for more militant action," he
said. "The clinics. Completely nonviolent, of course."

Samuel Lee volunteered to help organize the San Diego sit-ins.

At the Convention Center there was an unpleasant bit of news remaining for those delegates who had stayed for the final session. In the auditorium, the Reverend John Waddey announced that LAPAC had not withdrawn its suit against the Catholic dioceses after all. He urged the audience to go home and explain to anyone who would listen that the National Right to Life Committee and LAPAC were two different outfits, and that the NRLC had nothing to do with the suit, had nothing against the church. (Paul Brown later confirmed that the suit would, in fact, go forward. Brown explained that Sean Morton Downey had no authority to issue a statement without approval from the rest of the board. The following week, Mildred Jefferson would hold a press conference on the steps of the State House in Boston announcing that she was severing her ties with LAPAC.)

Dr. Jack Willke delivered the final charge to the NRLC delegates. His style was precisely that of a Rotarian firing up the troops for a fund-raising effort. The task at hand, he said, was working to elect pro-life politicians in the remaining primaries and the November elections. He did not mention any names, but he wore a Reagan button and he stressed the power of the presidency: "appointments to commissions, judicial appointments, particularly the Supreme Court." On the local level, he urged, "Don't just vote. Get in there and talk to the candidates. If they're goodies, support them at their meetings. And if they're bad guys and gals, picket them at their meetings . . ."

Willke asked the veteran members of the movement to search their souls: How long has it actually been since they had been out speaking to new audiences, looking for converts? "How long since you went out and showed the slides?" He said.

"Go *out* to those new people. *We* have the tools. *We* know how to change people's minds. We are so effective now that a number of times I've sat with a legislator for two hours and turned that person 180 degrees from a pro-abortion to a pro-life position and the legislator says, 'I never realized all of these things you are telling me.'" (Applause.)

Willke smiled. "Now, y'know, maybe I'm a little better at it than a few of you. But *with those pictures* . . ."

Epilogue

A movement defines itself by the goal it sets, and a measure of the integrity of that movement is the fidelity of its leaders to the letter and spirit of that goal. The goal of the right-to-life movement, as articulated in the various drafts of the proposed human life amendment supported by all major antiabortion groups, is the extension of constitutional protection to the unborn at all stages of development, including the zygote at the moment of fertilization. But in 1981, with their political power at an unprecedented level, some leaders of the movement began acting as though they were not concerned about every single zygote-person that might come into existence.

Following the inauguration of President Reagan, pro-choice groups including the National Abortion Rights Action League, Planned Parenthood, and the National Organization for Women intensified their attacks on the human life amendment. In newspaper advertisements and direct-mail fund-raising appeals, they stressed that the amendment would affect not only a woman's right to abortion, but to certain forms of birth control as well. The response of the National Right to Life Committee to these onslaughts was mildly schizophrenic. In the lead article of the March 9, 1981, *National Right to Life News*, "Physiologic Function of Certain Birth Control Measures," Dr. Jack C. Willke affirmed that, at least some of the time, the IUD, the standard birth control pill, and the so-called mini-pill, as well as prostaglandins and "morning-after" pills such as DES, all act as abortifacients. He left no doubt that, in his mind, such action was tantamount to murder. In describing the action of DES on a woman who had been impregnated during a rape, Willke wrote, "The drug had hardened the lining of the womb. About one week after fertilization, the multicelled tiny boy or girl could not implant and died. This mechanism was an abortion."

Less than three months later, attorney James Bopp, Jr., general counsel to the NRLC, indicated that perhaps such "abortions" were permissible, after all. On June 1, in another page-one article in the *National Right to Life News*—this one entitled "Effect of NRLC Human Life Amendment on Birth Control Drugs and Devices"—Bopp wrote:

> . . . as a practical matter, the Human Life Amendment, without supportive legislation, will only protect human beings known to be in existence. Those birth control drugs or devices whose action is, in whole or in part, abortifacient will not be directly affected by the passage of a Human Life Amendment if their action occurs prior to positive evidence of pregnancy.

Apparently Bopp was attempting to placate those who might oppose abortion but who do not oppose birth control. But his statement that the human life amendment would

have no effect on birth control without corroborative
legislation from the states was misleading. The HLA would
simply enable the legislatures to categorize abortions—at
any stage, from a third-trimester hysterotomy down to the
prevention of implantation by an IUD or pill—as crimes,
and to establish suitable penalties. In his eagerness to
dispute the charge that the NRLC was anti-birth control,
Bopp was clearly willing to sacrifice millions of fertilized
eggs—Dr. Willke's "tiny boys or girls." Under Bopp's interpretation of the HLA, an abortifacient drug or device
would be acceptable as long as its action occurred before
pregnancy could be detected. The deaths of millions of
zygote-people would be acceptable as long as nobody
knew when they were killed. Thus, in Bopp's analysis, the
notion that a fertilized egg deserves equal protection under
the law breaks down completely.

Others in the right-to-life movement might shrug; this
sort of compromise could be expected from the NRLC.
Hadn't it lionized Dr. Bernard Nathanson? Hadn't its
former president, Dr. Carolyn Gerster, seemed to approve
of the morning-after pill as a treatment for rape victims?
As we have seen, there is a spectrum of views within the
movement, and the NRLC is at what might be called the
liberal end of that spectrum. Not only is it flexible on the
issue of birth control, it is also reluctant to tie itself to the
New Right, and it refuses to become involved in other
right-wing issues such as pornography, homosexuality, and
sex education. Also, the NRLC supports a version of the
HLA that permits abortion to save the life of the mother,
rather than the so-called Paramount version which allows
no exceptions.

Further to the right are Paul Brown's Life Amendment

Political Action Committee and Judie Brown's American
Life Lobby. They are openly associated with the New
Right, they speak out on other "pro-family" issues, and
they support a no-exceptions HLA. In the March 1981
issue of the A.L.L. newsletter, LAPAC Administrative
Assistant James F. Kappus sought to establish the ideo-
logical purity of A.L.L. and LAPAC (at the expense of the
NRLC, which he did not mention):

> At the core of this broad circle called "pro-life" (like
> the sun to our solar system) is a nucleus of leaders who
> hold dear the principle that *ALL* human life is sacred
> from the moment of fertilization to the moment of
> natural death. Within this nucleus are the leaders who
> founded the movement and who continue to lead it
> closer to their stated goal of a *Paramount Human Life
> Amendment.*

But in the same newsletter there appeared a lengthy article
that actually backed away from the idea that abortion
should be treated as murder. This article, entitled "The
Human Life Amendment—What It Will Really Do," came
in response to the pro-choice charge that the HLA would
result in the outlawing of some birth control methods. In
it, the author, University of Notre Dame Law Professor
Charles Rice, acknowledges that under the HLA state legislatures could prohibit the manufacture and sale of abortifacients, but he dismisses the idea that women using such
abortifacients would be prosecuted for doing so. He also
argues, weakly, that abortion itself need not be classified
as murder under the HLA. "Let us be clear about one
thing," he begins. "Abortion is murder in the moral sense

because it is the directly intended taking of human life without justification." Yet, he says, this does not mean that it necessarily should be murder in the *legal* sense:

It is up to the legislature to determine the classifications and degrees of crimes which generally depend on extenuating circumstances and mental state of the defendant. Under the Human Life Amendment, the state legislatures would have flexibility in determining how abortion would be punished as it has such flexibility with respect to other unjustified killings.

Rice doesn't specify the "extenuating circumstances" or the "specific mental state of the defendant" that would classify abortion as a crime. He also doesn't clarify what he means by "other unjustified killings." Abortion is always premeditated; if the zygote/embryo/fetus is a person, then, barring an insanity ruling, abortion is first, or second, degree murder. Yet, apparently under pressure from the prochoice side, Rice, and by extension A.L.L. and LAPAC, have modified their position: what is murder in the moral sense need not be murder in the legal sense. So much for the ideological purity that James Kappus speaks about.

But perhaps the compassionate observer should view this backsliding with sympathy. Those who pledge allegiance to the wording of the human life amendment live in a surreal kingdom where the truths and everyday assumptions of life are harsh and demanding. In this kingdom, the life of a zygote produced in a mental institution by a paranoid schizophrenic man and a congenitally incompetent woman is sacred. So is the zygote inside the high school girl gang-raped by twelve college fraternity men, any one of whom could be the father. So is the zygote with Tay-Sachs disease, doomed to die after four years of suffering. It is little wonder that, in their efforts to persuade others to pledge fealty to the rule of the zygote-person-king, leading citizens of the kingdom would attempt to soften the edges, to blur the vision, as in the examples cited above. But in doing so they cast irrevocable doubt on the nature of their own quests, for the wording of the human life amendment is clear, and it demands total compliance.

Yet if we use James Kappus's analogy, there probably *is* a sun, a core of purity in the movement. It resides in the foothills of the Sierra Nevadas, in Coarsegold, California, with Elasah Drogin and her Catholics United for Life. These penitential warriors do not shrink from the gospel according to the HLA. For example, their newsletter dated Lent, 1981, contained an article entitled "Are Catholics Moral Cowards?," which began:

> Yes we are. Right down the street from the places where most of us live, worship, and work, babies are murdered by abortion—5,500 a day in the United States alone, and at least 4 times that many babies are killed by chemicals in the "pill" or by the IUD.

And later:

> We kill at least 30,000 babies a day in the United States. If we had a bloody house to house, hand to hand revolution in this country, it would be impossible to kill so many people. It is even more heart breaking when we realize that the 30,000 that die are innocent, unbaptized, and *needed!*

There is no dissembling here. There is no apologia stating that it is all right to kill zygote-people before they are able to prove their existence, no silly notions about separating what is moral from what should be legal. The IUD-induced death of a zygote-person, the abortion of a fetus-person, the killing of a man with a handgun all amount to the same thing—murder. The vision is pure.

Yet, even within the right-to-life movement—that is, within the Kingdom of the HLA—Catholics United for Life are sometimes considered extremists. They make the rest of the movement uncomfortable with their insistence that abortion *is* a Catholic issue, and with their claims that Catholic and fundamentalist Protestant clergy alike are not doing enough to eliminate abortion and artificial birth control. Precisely because of their extremism, they may be the only group capable of remaining intellectually and spiritually faithful to the cause of an inherently extremist movement. In the private context of such a movement, in a kingdom where zygotes are people and IUDs are murder weapons, it is only the extremists' extremists who see the pure, blinding truth.

Notes

Prologue

1. John T. Noonan, "A Private Choice," The Free Press, pp. 156-157.
2. Mary Anne Warren, "On the Moral and Legal Status of Abortion," anthologized in Wasserman, Richard A., "Today's Moral Problems," Second Edition, Macmillan, pp. 48-49.

Chapter 1: Birth Control and the Catholic Church

1. Quoted in *The New York Times*, August 8, 1963, p. 12.
2. *The New York Times*, December 15, 1959, p. 1.
3. *The New York Times*, April 11, 1960, p. 1.
4. *The New York Times*, July 30, 1968, p. 21.
5. *The New York Times*, August 6, 1963, p. 16.
6. *The New York Times*, August 5, 1963, p. 12.
7. Ibid.
8. *The New York Times*, August 11, 1968, p. 44.
9. Ibid.
10. *The New York Times*, July 19, 1969, p. 9.

11. *The New York Times*, November 16, 1966, p. 34.
12. *The New York Times*, July 30, 1968, p. 21.
13. Ibid., p. 1.

Chapter 2:   Of Bishops and Converts

1. *The New York Times*, January 22, 1969, p. 47.
2. *The New York Times*, January 8, 1968, p. 28.
3. *The New York Times*, March 23, 1966, p. 46.
4. *The New York Times*, February 22, 1967, p. 29.
5. *The New York Times*, February 25, 1967, p. 1.
6. *The New York Times*, March 9, 1967, p. 41.
7. *The New York Times*, April 26, 1967, p. 49.
8. *The New York Times*, December 8, 1969, p. 53.
9. Monroe, Keith, *The New York Times Magazine*, "How California's Abortion Law Isn't Working," December 29, 1968, p. 17.
10. Ibid.

Chapter 3:   New York—Abortion Capital of the Nation

1. *The New York Times*, November 25, 1978, p. 25.
2. *The New York Times*, September 16, 1971, p. 28.

Chapter 5:   The Catholic Church vs. the U.S. Supreme Court

1. *The New York Times*, January 24, 1973, p. 40.
2. *The New York Times*, January 23, 1973, p. 20.
3. Ibid.
4. *Constitution and the Church in the Modern World*, #51.
5. On November 5, 1981, the National Conference of Catholic Bishops changed its position on legislation

banning abortion. Conceding that the passage of a no-exceptions Human Life Amendment was unlikely, Cardinal Cooke and NCCB president Archbishop John P. Roach told a Senate Judiciary Subcommittee that they now backed a constitutional amendment which would simply empower Congress and individual states to legislate against abortion. Were such an amendment to pass, it is likely that some states would outlaw abortion while others would not. Under such a patchwork of laws, most moderately well off women would be able to travel to states where abortion remained legal, while most poor women would not. In effect, the bishops, eager to get something passed, shifted their support from a uniform antiabortion statute to one which would force only "poor" women to have babies or illegal abortions.

6. *The New York Times*, January 3, 1971, p. 36.
7. Ibid.
8. *The Boston Globe*, January 3, 1974, p. 18.
9. *The New York Times*, November 21, 1975, p. 19.

Chapter 6: Two Women from Texas

1. *The Boston Globe*, June 30, 1977, p. 21.
2. Ibid.

Chapter 7: "Thou Shalt Not Kill Zygotes"

1. FitzGerald, Frances, "A Disciplined, Charging Army," *The New Yorker*, May 18, 1981, p. 63.
2. Quoted in a promotional pamphlet for America's Pro Family Conference.

Chapter 10: Scenes from a Convention

1. *The Boston Globe*, June 10, 1981, p. 17.

Index